PIVOTAL
MOMENTS
IN HISTORY

THE FALL OF
CONSTANTINOPLE

RUTH TENZER FELDMAN

TFCB

TWENTY-FIRST CENTURY BOOKS
MINNEAPOLIS

To Marcia Marshall, editor extraordinaire

Consultant: Marios Philippides, professor of classics, University of Massachusetts, Amherst

Primary source material in this text is printed over an antique-paper texture.

The image on the jacket and cover shows the fall of Constantinople to the Ottoman Turks in 1453. This fresco, painted in 1537, decorates the outer wall of a monastery in Moldovita, Romania.

Twenty-First Century Books
A division of Lerner Publishing Group, Inc.
241 First Avenue North
Minneapolis, MN 55401 U.S.A.

Website address: www.lernerbooks.com

Library of Congress Cataloging-in-Publication Data

Feldman, Ruth Tenzer.
    The fall of Constantinople / by Ruth Tenzer Feldman.
        p.   cm. — (Pivotal moments in history)
    Includes bibliographical references and index.
    ISBN 978–0–8225–5918–4 (lib. bdg. : alk. paper)
    1. Byzantine Empire—History—Juvenile literatue. 2. Istanbul (Turkey)—History—
Siege, 1453—Juvenile literature. I. Title.
    DF504.5.F45 2008
    949.5'04—dc22   2006037501

Manufactured in the United States of America
1 2 3 4 5 6 – DP – 13 12 11 10 09 08

CONTENTS

CHAPTER ONE
No place more worthy

As avid of fame as Alexander of Macedon . . . [Mehmed II]

says times have changed, so that he would go from the

East to the West, as the Westerners had gone to the East.

The Empire of the world, he says, must be one, one faith

and one kingdom. To make this unity there is no place in

the world more worthy than Constantinople.

—*writer and merchant Giacomo de' Languschi, 1453*

About 560 years ago, a Venetian merchant named Giacomo de' Languschi met a young Turkish leader named Mehmed II. Mehmed spoke frankly about his idol, Alexander the Great, who in 336 B.C. set out to conquer the world. Mehmed boasted that he and Alexander were very much alike.

Like Alexander the Great, Mehmed was about twenty years old when he rose to power. Alexander's father Philip, king of the Macedonians, had tried in vain to capture a fortified city called Byzantion in 339 B.C. In the early fifteenth century, Mehmed's father, sultan of the Ottomans, tried to conquer the same city, then called Constantinople (modern Istanbul, Turkey). He also failed. Mehmed was determined to seize this city, called the Gate of Happiness and the Eye of the World, and then, like Alexander, go on to rule a vast empire.

A PERFECT SPOT

For centuries many people thought that this "eye of the world" was the most perfect spot on Earth. The city sits on a hilly peninsula with a natural harbor that shelters ships from strong winds and the treacherous currents of the Bosporus Strait, a narrow waterway separating Europe from Asia and linking the Sea of Marmara south of the peninsula with the Black Sea to its north. With many rivers emptying into it, the Black Sea is a key center for transportation to the interior of Europe and Asia. In modern times, the Black Sea provides ports for Bulgaria, Romania, Ukraine, Russia, Georgia, and Turkey. A waterway once called the Hellespont (the modern-day Dardanelles) connects the Sea of Marmara with the Aegean Sea and the Mediterranean, providing ports for southern Europe, North Africa, and the Middle East.

Legend tells us that about 650 B.C. Greek colonists from a town near Athens discovered how advantageous it would be to settle on this hilly peninsula. They were led by a man named Byzas, and they called the site Byzantion in his honor. Once fortified by walls, the peninsula was easily defended. Its excellent deepwater harbor—an inlet called the Golden Horn—invited trade from all over the known world. Products from as far away as Iceland could be found on the merchant ships anchored there. The leaders of Byzantion collected tolls from ships passing through Bosporus Strait, and the city grew wealthy.

Persia (present-day Iran), the Greek city-states of Sparta and Athens, and the Roman Empire sought to control the city. Rome conquered it in A.D. 193. Its name was changed to the Latin form—Byzantium. A Roman emperor rebuilt the city to about twice its original size.

By A.D. 312, the Roman Empire covered so much territory that it was split in two. A group of leaders in Rome governed the western half, while another group in Byzantium ruled the eastern half. Constantine, the son of a Roman emperor, defeated a rival army to become ruler of the western half of the Roman Empire.

According to legend, he credited his victory to a vision telling him to fight under the banner of a Christian cross. For ten years, he ruled the western half of the empire jointly with the leader of the empire's eastern half.

Then Constantine

This bronze statue of Constantine I is in York, England, which was part of the western Roman Empire when Constantine was named emperor in A.D. 306.

In 325 Constantine (center, background) oversaw the first meeting of Christian religious leaders in Nicaea, Turkey. The gathering was known as the First Council of Nicaea. During Constantine's rule, Christians gained freedom of worship, and the religion grew and flourished.

overthrew the eastern ruler and declared himself absolute ruler of a reunited Roman Empire. Constantine chose Byzantium, rather than Rome, as the empire's new capital.

Although Constantine would not formally convert to Christianity until right before his death, he declared that Byzantium would be dedicated to Christian religion and culture. Christianity, which had been suppressed in the Roman Empire, became the city's official religion. In 325 Constantine brought together leaders of the Christian Church for a council in Nicaea (present-day Iznik, Turkey). Council members drew up a statement of beliefs, known as the Nicene Creed. Some Christians accepted these beliefs. Others did not. Despite Constantine's efforts to create a united Christian Church, the eastern and western churches became more and more divided over doctrine and religious practices.

In 326 Constantine began building a magnificent cathedral, called the Church of Holy Wisdom (in Greek, "Hagia Sophia"), as the religious center for Christians in his empire. After the cathedral was completed, he officially renamed Byzantium New Rome on May 11, 330. New Rome soon began to be called Constantinople—Constantine's City—or, simply, the City.

The Visigoths, a Germanic tribe from the Black Sea region, overran Rome in 410 and invaded lands farther west, including Gaul (France). Soon after this, the people of Constantinople enclosed their city with a stronger set of fortifications. They built three sets of walls with moats in between them and 192 watchtowers. In 443 these walls protected Constantinople from attacks by Attila, a leader of the Huns—an Asiatic tribe that overran much of Europe. Invasions by other tribes brought the collapse of the Roman Empire in the west in 476, but Constantinople's walls protected the city against invasion for the next one thousand years.

THE DARK AGES

After the fall of the Roman Empire in the West, regions formerly controlled by Rome fought one another for dominance. From roughly 500 to 1000, once known as the Dark Ages and currently often called the Early Middle Ages, few advances were made in the arts and sciences and some skills were forgotten. Scholarship continued behind the walls of Constantinople, though, and the Roman Empire in the East flourished.

JUSTINIAN'S EMPIRE

The Eastern Roman Empire, or what we call the Byzantine Empire, expanded to the east and west of Constantinople. During the reign of its emperor Justinian, from 527 to 565, the empire expanded to stretch from the Euphrates River (in Iraq) across northern Africa to the Strait of Gibraltar at the western end of the Mediterranean Sea. It included virtually all of Italy and extended throughout the Middle East.

Justinian, who was a military leader, began his reign as coemperor with his uncle, Justin. After his uncle's death, Justinian ruled Byzantium jointly with his wife, Theodora.

Emperor Justinian I (left) and his wife, Empress Theodora (right), ruled Byzantium from 527 to 565. They are immortalized in mosaics (images created from tiny color tiles) found in the western Italian city of Ravenna, which Justinian conquered in 540. Ravenna became the seat of Byzantine government in Italy.

She was an intelligent and strong-willed woman whose parents had been entertainers. Theodora also had a reputation for beauty and sexual appetites.

Justinian decided to revise the complex and contradictory tangle of Roman laws that governed his empire. The Roman legal system was divided into the "old laws"—which dated back hundreds of years—and the "new laws"—which contained more recent rules and interpretations. The emperor instructed Tribonian, his quaestor (attorney general, or high legal officer) to meet with a panel of experts and rewrite the laws.

In 529 the panel of experts produced a ten-volume set of revised laws called the Codex, which would apply throughout the empire. The introduction to the Codex stated that the maxims of law are to live honestly, hurt no one, and give everyone his due. The citizens of Constantinople often disagreed about what this meant in the day-to-day life of the empire.

Constantinople's citizens were originally divided into four demes, or self-governing groups. Each group had civic duties, such as repairing the city walls or working in the public gardens. The four demes gradually reorganized into two—the Greens and the Blues. These were the colors worn by the two main teams of charioteers who raced against each other in the city's large arena, the Hippodrome, during the reign of Justinian and Theodora.

The Hippodrome was first built more than three hundred years before the reign of Justinian. It was enlarged by Constantine to about 1,500 feet (457 meters) long and 400 feet (122 m) wide, and it could seat about sixty thousand people.

The Hippodrome was crowded with spectators on January 13, 532, when Justinian appeared to start the races. Justinian had spent vast amounts of money on buildings and lavish entertainment. He financed these projects with high taxes and a corrupt system of extorting money from the wealthy. The people of Constantinople became increasingly angry about the corruption.

As usual, the crowds at the Hippodrome that day yelled *nika!* (win). But instead of cheering for their favorite teams, they cheered on a revolt against the emperor's repressive ways.

A Roman triptych (three-paneled artwork) from the fifth century A.D. shows a senator and his family watching chariot races in the Hippodrome.

For five days, a popular uprising known as the Nika Revolt raged through the city. Rioters captured the Hippodrome, released everyone in the city's prison, set fire

STAY AND FIGHT!

During the Nika Revolt in 532, Emperor Justinian hid in his palace and planned to flee Constantinople. The empress Theodora scornfully told him that imperial purple robes made a worthy cover for the dead.

"[H]ow could an Emperor ever allow himself to be a fugitive?" she asked. "If you, my lord, wish to save your skin, you will have no difficulty in doing so. As for me, I stand by the ancient saying: the purple is the noblest winding sheet."

Justinian found two generals who organized their troops and slaughtered the mob surrounding the palace.

to the prison and other buildings, crowned their own emperor (an elderly man from a royal family), and stormed the royal palace. Justinian wanted to flee the city, but Theodora convinced him to stay and fight. Eventually Justinian roused his army, which killed thirty thousand to fifty thousand people and ended the uprising. Theodora insisted that the people's emperor be executed.

About a month after the revolt was crushed, Justinian began plans to construct a new Hagia Sophia, more magnificent than the one built by Constantine two hundred years earlier. Because of the riots, much of the city needed rebuilding too, and Justinian saw to those repairs as well. But he was determined that Hagia Sophia would be his crowning achievement.

And it was. The new church took nearly six years to build. A huge central dome rises above its square walls. Gold-flecked mosaics covered walls and ceilings. Artwork from throughout the empire was incorporated into the building. It was said that a team of five thousand workers on the north side competed with five thousand workers on the south side and that the construction cost 320,000 pounds (145,000 kilograms) of gold. During the church's dedication, around Christmas 537, Justinian was said to have compared himself to King Solomon, who built a temple in Jerusalem in biblical times. He murmured, "Solomon, I have surpassed thee."

After the rebuilding projects, Constantinople was once again a bustling, thriving city, at the very heart of the trade routes between East and West. One of the empire's most prized products was silk from Asia, and the emperor's family and other noble families held a monopoly on the trade in silk.

According to legend, in about 550, two Christian monks arrived in Constantinople from China, bringing with them a hollowed-out staff filled with silkworm eggs and seeds for mulberry trees, since mulberry leaves are the main diet of silkworms. They also brought the secret of making silk, a secret the Chinese had guarded for millennia. Byzantium soon began to manufacture its own silken textiles, which were exported throughout Europe.

LIFE IN THE CITY

Constantinople drew people from many parts of the empire in Europe, North Africa, and Asia. Rich and poor lived close to one another. The brick homes of the wealthy were usually at least two stories high—in order to have a view of the sea. They often had a central courtyard featuring fruit trees or a fountain and a special room where women could be secluded from male company. Women who lived in the city were expected to stay at home most of the time. When they did venture out to church or the public bathhouses, they kept their heads covered and faces veiled. Bathhouses had a long history in the Roman Empire. They provided places where men and, in a separate area, women could get together for cleaning and conversation.

Houses of the poor were less well constructed. Many families crowded into poorly ventilated tenements sometimes ten stories high. Laws forbade these structures from blocking their wealthier neighbors' view of the sea.

City officials regulated how wide a street could be, the cost of goods, hours of work, the drainage of water and sewage into the sea, and other aspects of daily living. Government buildings and palaces at the eastern end of the city were connected to other parts of town by the Middle Way (*mese*), which was lined with shops.

The poorer men and women in the city, like those living in rural areas, usually wore simple cotton, linen, or woolen tunics of varying lengths, belted at the waist, with a woolen cloak for colder weather. Wealthier men wore another loose-fitting garment over their tunics. Upper-class women in Justinian's time wore long garments with full-length sleeves and loose cloaks with elaborate designs. They also wore jewelry, often a pendant that had a Christian image or inscription.

During Justinian's reign, the poor received free bread. They could enjoy the large public gardens and had free admission to public circuses featuring trained bears and acrobats. A city official was assigned to supervise orphanages.

Slavery was an accepted institution. Slaves made bricks, pottery, textiles, baskets, and jewelry or served in palaces or the private homes of the wealthy. Slaves could be captives in war or people who fell into debt. They sometimes were able to work their way to freedom.

Eunuchs—men who were infertile because their testicles were removed—were highly valued in Byzantine society. Eunuchs were allowed to mix freely with women. They could become the highest-ranking religious leader—the patriarch—and hold any important military or political office except emperor. Boys of the upper classes might be made eunuchs to gain a powerful position in society.

Constantinople had at least one university and several schools. There is no record of girls attending schools, although some women were taught privately and did acquire an education. Boys first attended school at about the age of six, when they began to memorize portions of the Christian Bible and works by the ancient Greek poet Homer. They later studied arithmetic, astronomy, geometry, literature, music, and science. In their teens, they might study law, medicine, and physics.

Even though Justinian was considered the leader of the Roman Empire and the language of ancient Rome was Latin, the more common language in Constantinople and the one most thoroughly taught in schools was Greek. After the death of Justinian, the emperor was called the *basileus*, the old Greek name for a king. The people of Byzantium held on to their ancient Greek heritage, and Constantinople gradually became less Roman. Although Constantinople was considered a Christian city, the Greeks studied and preserved literary works by scholars living in the pre-Christian era. Many of these works have formed the basis of present-day classical studies.

By the end of the sixth century, Constantinople had added another fortification to prevent ships from sailing into the Golden Horn. They chained together a huge line of logs and stretched this floating boom across the Golden Horn, from Constantinople to the watchtower (known then as the Tower of Christ) that had been built in the settlement of Galata (also called Pera) on the other side of the harbor.

GALATA/PERA

Just north of the Golden Horn, opposite the walled city of Constantinople, was a trading port that developed quite differently from its Greek neighbor across the harbor. Galata/Pera might have been inhabited by Celtic people, members of a northern European tribe that sacked Rome around 390 B.C. and moved eastward into present-day Turkey. They settled in a region that was later called Galatia in the Christian Bible. These people had milk white skin (*galakt* is a Greek word for "milk") and red hair. Pera—another name for the area—comes from an ancient Greek description of the area as being on the other side of or beyond Constantinople. Genoese merchants took control of Galata/Pera in the twelfth century, and the city prospered.

THE BIRTH OF ISLAM

A few years after the death of Byzantine emperor Justinian I in 565, the prophet Muhammad was born in Mecca (in present-day Saudi Arabia). According to his followers, after Muhammad experienced a revelation of God through the angel Gabriel, he began to spread the teachings of God ("Allah" in Arabic). The name of the religion Muhammad taught is Islam, which means "submission to God" in Arabic. Islam's holy book, the Quran, teaches Muslims (followers of Islam) how to lead a life committed to a just society under God's laws. Islam is a monotheistic (belief in a single deity) religion that shares roots with Judaism and Christianity.

During Muhammad's lifetime, Byzantium and Persia competed for control of much of the Middle East. Persia captured Jerusalem in 614 and seized many sacred Christian relics. Byzantine emperor Heraclius vowed to reclaim the relic and restore Jerusalem to Christian—and Byzantine—rule. He fought his way toward the Persian capital of Ctesiphon (ruins remain in present-day Salman Pak, Iraq). Meanwhile, the Persian army mounted an unsuccessful attack on Constantinople. Verses in the Quran mention these wars, and tradition says that Muhammad sent a letter to Byzantine emperor Heraclius and Persia's King Chosroes II inviting them to convert to Islam.

The first people who embraced Islam lived in the Arabian Peninsula. By the time of Muhammad's death in 632, many people there had become Muslims. The Muslim Arabs who left for other regions in the Middle East took their new faith with them. They gained power through alliances and combat, while Persia and Byzantium weakened

Byzantium and Persia fought each other for control of the Middle East during Heraclius's reign. This illuminated manuscript from 626 depicts Persians attacking Constantinople.

each other militarily. Heraclius managed to return the holy relics stolen by the Persians to Jerusalem in 629, but Arab forces defeated his army in Syria in 636. By 639 Jerusalem was under Muslim control, as well as important ports in Egypt that had been under Byzantine control. A few years later, Persia became part of the Islamic empire.

As Islam continued to spread, the Arab Muslims became divided over who should be the successor to Muhammad, or caliph (*khalifah* means "successor" in Arabic). Rival caliphates (territories ruled by a caliph) vied with one another for power. Baghdad, the capital of the Abbasid caliphate, became a leading city in the Muslim world.

Muslims tried repeatedly to conquer Constantinople but failed to breach the heavily fortified walls encircling the city. One siege began in 672 with a naval blockade and lasted nearly five years. The Byzantines sprayed the enemy ships with napalmlike Greek fire, which finally destroyed most of the fleet.

GREEK FIRE

When Arab ships sailed into the Sea of Marmara in 674, they were met with a secret weapon called Greek fire. This flammable liquid was probably a mixture of sulfur, naphtha, and lime. It was similar to napalm used in twentieth-century warfare.

Although flammable liquids had been used in war for about one thousand years before the Muslim siege of Constantinople, the Byzantines used Greek fire in a most deadly fashion. They projected it through bronze tubes mounted on ships and the defense walls. Greek fire floated on the water and clung to whatever it touched, setting people and wooden-hulled ships ablaze.

A Syrian refugee named Kallinikos might have developed Greek fire for the Byzantines. Its secret was so secure that eventually the Byzantines forgot how to make it. Greek fire was used against a second Muslim naval attack in 717 but rarely after that.

This illustration of the Byzantine navy using Greek fire is from the Madrid Skylitzes illuminated manuscript, a twelth-century version of the Synopsis Historian, *a history of the Byzantine empire by Joannes (John) Skylitzes.*

In this fourteenth-century fresco from a monastery in present-day Macedonia, brothers Cyril and Methodius are shown with scrolls written in Cyrillic—a system of writing that captured the spoken language of the Slavic region. Latin and Greek were the traditional languages used to preach the Christian faith.

CONQUEST AND CONVERTS

While Islam spread into India, North Africa, and Spain, Byzantium's Christians gained converts among neighboring Slavic regions. In the 860s, two brothers—Cyril and Methodius—preached the Christian faith to Moravians (a people living in present-day Czech Republic) in their own language, rather than in Latin or Greek. The mission was supported by the patriarch of Constantinople. This caused conflict with the pope, since the Roman Catholic Church required that religious ceremonies be conducted in Latin. Cyril is credited as developing the Cyrillic alphabet, which captures the sounds of the Slavic languages in a written form.

By 900 Byzantium had established churches throughout the Balkan region and started to trade with a collection of non-Christian tribes of Rus (Russians). In the late tenth century, Vladimir, the ruler of the Rus city of Kiev, decided his people should have a single religion. The envoys he sent to Constantinople reported that "the Greeks led us to the edifices where they worship their God, and we knew not whether we were in heaven or on earth . . . We only know that God dwells there among men."

Byzantine emperor Basil II secured a military alliance with the Rus by offering his sister Anna in marriage to Vladimir. Vladimir later came to Basil's aid and claimed his bride. Chronicles at the time wrote that Vladimir forcibly baptized all the people of Kiev in the Dnieper River in a single day.

An illuminated manuscript from Russia known as the Radziwill Chronicle depicts the baptism of Rus ruler Vladimir in 988. Vladimir converted his entire people to Christianity.

The Bulgarians and later the Serbs also adopted Orthodoxy, the Christianity practiced in Constantinople, rather than the Roman or Latin Christianity of the western region. The common religion between Bulgaria and Byzantium still did not prevent warfare. Basil was determined to destroy Bulgaria and rid Byzantium of an enemy on its western doorstep.

Basil earned the name Bulgar-Slayer in 1014. Bulgaria's ruler attacked Constantinople in an attempt to gain control of the city. Basil's army defeated the Bulgarian forces and captured nearly fifteen thousand Bulgarian soldiers. He ordered that ninety-nine Bulgars out of every hundred be blinded. The hundredth soldier was blinded in only one eye, so that he could lead his comrades home.

There was a less brutal side to Basil too. Traveling through his kingdom, he heard thousands of reports about the upper classes seizing property belonging to poor farmers. With this in mind, he wrote a law to redistribute property throughout the empire. Under Basil's law, all estates that were established before the reign of Basil's grandfather would remain untouched. But "estates acquired since . . . shall be considered to be illegally owned. . . . The peasants, the original owners, who were long since expelled by the owners of the large estates, have the right to reclaim . . . their property without being required to repay the sales price, or to pay for any improvements which may have been installed by the proprietors who are about to be dispossessed."

A few years after Basil II died in 1025, the new emperor of Byzantium, Constantine VIII, repealed the laws that had helped peasants retain their property. Tensions continued to grow between the rich landowners and the poor. Internal problems were matched by trouble between Byzantium and her neighbors.

Byzantium's borders shrank and grew, depending on the strength of the emperor's armies and those of other regional rulers eager to expand their territory. These included Slavic leaders from the Balkans as well as Arabs who controlled the Mediterranean islands of Crete and Sicily.

By this time, Arab Muslims had established thriving communities in Spain and created a

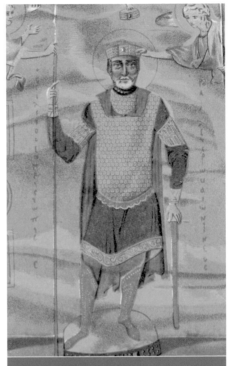

Basil II, the Bulgar-Slayer, ruled Byzantium from 976 until his death in 1025. This illustration is based on the illuminated title page of Basil II's psalter (a volume containing the biblical Book of Psalms) made during his reign.

caliphate there that rivaled the one in Baghdad. Another caliph ruled over much of northern Africa from his imperial headquarters in Cairo. At the same time, many nomadic tribes in central Asia had become Muslim and were gradually moving west. These tribes, according to Chinese chroniclers from about 500 B.C., had their homeland in the hilly region north of Manchuria. They were called the Tu-kueh—the Turks.

Among the prominent tribes were the Seljuk Turks. Their leaders had converted to Islam at about the time that the Rus had converted to the Greek Orthodox religion of Byzantium. The Seljuks migrated into Persia and adopted much of the Persian language and culture. They gained more and more territory, first by siding with various factions during power struggles among the Persians and later in a decisive battle in 1039 against the ruling Persian family.

Having consolidated their forces in Persia, the Seljuks were ready to move westward into Anatolia (part of present-day Turkey). Anatolia is the western-most peninsula of Asia, also known as Asia Minor. The Seljuks were still mostly nomads and probably occupied land that wasn't already being farmed. They were generally not destructive conquerors and lived in relative peace with the other Turkic tribes in the region. Still, Seljuk expansion began to threaten the Byzantine Empire. Anatolia's fertile grain fields had made it the breadbasket of Byzantium, and the men of Anatolia had filled the ranks of the emperor's army.

THE WIDENING FISSURE WITH ROME

While Byzantium's leaders worked to improve the military and economic might of the empire—and fought one another to gain the imperial throne—the rifts between two major sects of the Christian faith continued to widen. In the six hundred years since the destruction of the Western Roman Empire, Greek had replaced Latin as the language of the Byzantine churches, which were governed by the patriarch in Constantinople. The pope remained the religious authority for the churches in Rome and many parts of western Europe, where Latin was still used in church services. The patriarchs and the popes continued to argue over who should control churches throughout the Balkan region, which lay between them.

Conflicts over Christian doctrine had prompted the first emperor of Constantinople (Constantine I) to convene a council of bishops in 325. Subsequent emperors were also caught up in religious controversies—and their social and political ramifications. One divisive issue involved a biblical prohibition against idol worship.

In 726 through 729, Byzantine emperor Leo III issued edicts outlawing the making of icons—images of God, Jesus, or the Greek Orthodox saints that people kept in their homes or at their churches. The edict limited church decoration to images of plain crosses or plants and animals. He ordered iconoclasts—image breakers—to destroy the religious mosaics and other icons that had been carefully crafted and honored throughout the empire.

The patriarch of Constantinople and people in the western part of the empire refused to obey the emperor, and many who tried to preserve the mosaics were imprisoned or executed. Leo III also retaliated against Pope Gregory III, who opposed the iconoclastic edict. The emperor transferred regions in southern Italy from the jurisdiction of the pope to that of the patriarch of Constantinople. This deprived the pope of followers and financial resources. More than one hundred years later, a church council in Constantinople once again allowed the popular practice of honoring icons.

Conflicts over Christian doctrine came to a head in 1054. The head of the Orthodox Church in Constantinople, Patriarch Michael I Cerularius, had written a letter to Pope Leo IX condemning certain practices of the Roman Church. For instance, Western churches used unleavened bread (bread made without yeast) in their Mass (the main worship service). The Eastern churches use leavened bread or leavened bread dipped in wine.

Three delegates from Pope Leo IX visited Constantinople and brought with them the pope's written response to the patriarch's letter. They did not deliver it right away. Meanwhile, news came to Constantinople that the pope had died. Still, the delegates stayed and argued with the patriarch over church doctrine. Both sides refused to yield.

Finally, the delegates strode into Hagia Sophia with the pope's letter. It was a bull (official announcement) of excommunication that expelled the patriarch of Constantinople from the Christian Church. Soon afterward, Patriarch Michael I excommunicated the three delegates (since there was no pope to excommunicate) in return.

This break between the two branches of Christianity in 1054 became known as the Great Schism (split). It was the result of tensions that had existed over the centuries, almost since the founding of the faith. And it would influence the fate of Byzantium—and the Middle East—for centuries.

A Greek manuscript written in the fifteenth century depicts Pope Leo IX (left) excommunicating Patriarch Michael I Cerularius (right), causing the Great Schism, the split between the Orthodox Church and the Roman Catholic Church.

CHAPTER TWO
Discord, decline, and destruction

And so began the war.

—*Geoffrey of Villehardouin*
(French crusader), December 1203

Constantinople faced difficult times in the decades following the Great Schism. In 1055 the Seljuk Turks captured
Baghdad and continued to amass a powerful army. That
same year, Norman invaders captured Bari, the last
Byzantine territory in Italy. The Normans were a mixture of
French, German, and Viking peoples. They had settled in
northern France around 900 and soon began moving into
other territory throughout Europe. In 1066 the army of

William II, duke of Normandy, conquered England.

In 1071 the Byzantine army, most of whom were mercenaries (paid fighters), gathered in Anatolia to stop an advancing army of Seljuk Turks who had gained control of Armenia and were moving toward Constantinople. Emperor Romanus IV Diogenes, a former general, divided his army in two. He took half his men (about thirty-five thousand) to capture the small fortress town of Manzikert in Anatolia. The next day, in a skirmish with the Seljuks, several units of Turkish mercenaries abandoned the emperor's army. The Seljuk leader Alp Arslan offered a truce. He had originally moved his forces into the territory to control renegade Turkish tribes, not to attack Byzantium. But Romanus refused the offer. He expected reinforcements of about thirty-five thousand more men to arrive soon.

The battle at Manzikert began. The reinforcements Romanus was waiting for never came, perhaps through a

Seljuk leader Alp Arslan (seated) *ruled over the Turks from 1064 to 1072. He led the Turks into battle against Byzantine emperor Romanus IV Diogenes in 1071.*

An eleventh-century illuminated manuscript, written by Greek historian Ioannes (John) Skylitzes, contains this illustration of a battle between Byzantine and Seljuk cavalry (soldiers on horseback).

mistake or perhaps because of political intrigue among Byzantine officials who wanted to overthrow Romanus. Soon other portions of the army deserted. One eyewitness described the scene of battle this way: "It was like an earthquake: the shouting, the sweat, the swift rushes of fear, the clouds of dust, and not least the hordes of Turks riding all around us. . . . What indeed could be more pitiable than to see the entire imperial army in flight . . . and knowing that the Empire itself was on the verge of collapse?"

Romanus stood his ground, was captured, and was later brought before Alp Arslan, who treated him well. The two leaders signed a peace treaty, and Romanus returned to Constantinople.

Rivals to the throne captured the defeated emperor. They blinded Romanus—under Byzantine law a blind person was considered unfit to rule—and sent him into exile, where he died in 1072. Alp Arslan died that year as well.

Although a relatively small conflict in terms of lives lost, the battle at Manzikert was the worst blow suffered by Byzantium in more than seven hundred years. The new emperor, Michael VII, refused to honor the treaty between Romanus and the Seljuks. About a year later, the Seljuks conquered most of Anatolia. Byzantium was able to keep a part of western Anatolia but lost the territory from which it had received most of its grain and its manpower.

As their empire grew, the Seljuks established a capital in the Anatolian city of Konya (Iconium). Since Anatolia had once been in the eastern part of the Byzantine (Roman) Empire, Turkish people who lived there were known as the Rum Seljuks. *Rum* is the Arabic word for "Rome." They governed most of their territory indirectly, through alliances with local potentates (people in power). Anatolia was slowly changing from a predominantly Christian to a predominantly Muslim area. Isolated groups of Armenians who had their own Orthodox Christian practices survived in the mountainous regions. Other Christian communities held on in coastal areas along the Black Sea and the Mediterranean.

CAUGHT BETWEEN EAST AND WEST

Despite clashes with the Church of Rome, crushing defeats by the Seljuk Turks, and internal dissension that bordered on civil war, Byzantium, the Byzantine Empire, managed to survive. Alexius I Comnenus became emperor in 1081 and started to reclaim territory for the empire. Alexius I was the first of several members of the Comnenus dynasty to rule Byzantium.

Alexius I allowed the pope to use Constantinople as a stopover for armies of crusaders. These knights and commoners from western Europe vowed to fight for the Church of Rome and capture Jerusalem and surrounding areas from Muslim control. Alexius thought that the crusader army would be a few hundred well-trained knights who would battle the Seljuk Turks in Anatolia before continuing to the Middle East. Instead, the crusaders who arrived in Constantinople around 1095 were mainly a ragtag collection of people who looted and destroyed wherever they stopped to make camp. The Byzantines didn't delay in ferrying them across to Anatolia. The Turks soon massacred many of them.

A few years later, however, the Seljuk Turks were no longer as united and powerful a fighting force. Despite their skills in administering a large empire, the Seljuks still followed the traditional inheritance custom among nomads. When a family leader died, his land and property were divided among surviving sons, brothers, or nephews. This tradition resulted in smaller, less powerful states with less influence or in war among the inheritors to get a larger share. Another crusade was organized and succeeded in recapturing Jerusalem. Byzantium regained some of its former territory as well.

In the next century, the Byzantine Empire continued to be plagued by debt and corrupt government. Powerful local landowners and foreign merchants—particularly Venetians— controlled much of the empire's wealth. Venice, a city-state at the northern end of the Adriatic Sea, had built a large shipyard and naval station in the early twelfth century. Venetian merchants, backed by a powerful navy, made profitable trade agreements throughout the Adriatic and Mediterranean regions. Many Venetians who came to Constantinople for business bought estates and stayed on to enjoy Byzantine art, music, and literature.

Manuel I Comnenus tried to control the Venetian merchants in Constantinople but failed. This portrait of Manuel and his second wife, Maria of Antioch, appears in a Vatican (the seat of the Roman Catholic Church) manuscript.

In 1171 Byzantine emperor Manuel I Comnenus arrested more than ten thousand Venetians in one day and tried to take away their property and trading privileges. He claimed that the Venetians had attacked Galata/Pera, across the Golden Horn. Many of the residents of Galata/Pera were from Genoa, another Italian city-state and a rival of Venice for influence and trade. Manuel I was later forced by Venice to free the merchants.

Manuel I died in 1180, soon after marrying off his ten-year-old son, Alexius II, to a nine-year-old princess from France. But Manuel's cousin, Andronicus Comnenus, staged a military coup, claiming the throne as rightfully his. He killed Alexius and his mother and took the young princess, then twelve, as his bride. Andronicus spent much of his reign killing or imprisoning those he thought might want to take the throne from him. He sent a guard to arrest his cousin, Isaac II Angelus, but in 1185 Isaac killed the guard and rallied the people to revolt. When the revolt succeeded, they subjected Andronicus to a slow and tortuous death.

The people of Constantinople soon discovered that they had exchanged a cruel emperor for a corrupt one. The Angelus family produced three emperors whose actions proved disastrous for Constantinople. Shortly after Isaac II took power, his younger brother made a grab for the throne. In 1195 that brother, Alexius III Angelus, blinded and imprisoned Isaac and crowned himself emperor. He allowed Isaac's teenage son, known as young Alexius, to leave the empire.

During the struggles between the Comnenus and Angelus families in Constantinople, Christian and Muslim armies continued to battle for control of Jerusalem. In 1187 Saladin (or Salah al-Din), a Kurdish Muslim military leader from present-day Iraq, took Jerusalem from crusader forces. Saladin's victory is one of the major turning points in the history of the Crusades. Within a few years, Saladin's empire covered much of the Middle East and his influence spread to Constantinople. Officials there erected a mosque in his honor for the Muslims who lived in the city.

The fall of Jerusalem prompted the Third Crusade (1189–1192), financed largely by a special Saladin tithe (a church offering of 10 percent of income) in England. French, German, and English soldiers recaptured part of Saladin's empire. England's king, Richard the Lion-Hearted,

This illustration from a fifteenth-century collection of songs by French composer Loyset Compère shows the conquest of Jerusalem by Saladin I in 1187.

and Saladin signed a treaty allowing Christians to visit Jerusalem, which would remain under Muslim control.

THE FATEFUL FOURTH CRUSADE

After Saladin died in 1193, his relatives divided the realm among them, and it soon seemed vulnerable. Seizing the opportunity to retake Jerusalem, Pope Innocent III called for Christians to wage another holy war to wrest control of Jerusalem from the Muslim "infidels" (unbelievers). In 1199 knights, foot soldiers, and commoners—about eight thousand to ten thousand crusaders—gathered at Ecry, France.

Among the leaders was Count Baldwin of Flanders (part of Belgium), a twenty-eight-year-old vassal (or subject) of the king of France. Baldwin's wife, Marie, also pledged to support the crusade. She was the sister of Count Thibaut of Champagne (France), another key figure in the campaign. One of Thibaut's commanders, Geoffrey of Villehardouin, kept a chronicle of events. Historians have learned many of the details of this Fourth Crusade from his chronicle.

The crusade leaders decided to launch a naval attack on ports in Egypt and then make their way to Jerusalem. They sent six envoys to Italy to find warships, sailors, and supplies. In 1201 the envoys signed a treaty with Venice to provide enough ships by June 1202 to transport 33,500 crusaders and forty-five hundred horses to the Middle East. The treaty called for the crusaders to pay eighty-five thousand silver "marks of Cologne" (coins) by April 1202. They provided only two thousand marks to the Venetians as a down payment.

These preparations were a huge undertaking. For months Venetian shipbuilders devoted nearly all their energies to filling the order for the crusaders. The ships and crew were ready on time in June 1202, as the crusader army began arriving and setting up camp just outside Venice. But soon it became clear that the envoys had overestimated the number of men joining the crusade. The fighting force was only about eleven thousand, not thirty-three thousand. Worse still, the knights and nobles didn't have enough money to pay the Venetians what was owed.

Although they wanted the money due them before they let the crusaders sail away, the Venetians did not want an unruly army on their doorstep. Doge (Duke) Enrico Dandolo, the old, blind leader of the Venetian council, came up with a solution.

Dandolo proposed that Venice would get about one-half of the booty captured during the crusade and that the crusaders would go off to war as quickly as possible. On its way to Egypt, the crusader fleet would help the Venetians threaten Zara, a port on the Adriatic Sea that was controlled by the king of Hungary. Hungary was a trade rival of Venice.

Zara was a predominately Christian city, which caused some crusader leaders to question the morality of their mission. But Dandolo led them to believe that the people of Zara would immediately surrender at the sight of so large a force. The fleet could then wait out the winter in Zara and set sail again in the spring. The crusader leaders agreed.

When crusader and Venetian warships reached Zara in early November 1202, the people of that city refused to surrender. The crusaders joined the

The old, blind Venetian doge Enrico Dandolo attacked Zara, a port on the Adriatic Sea. This sixteenth-century painting of the attack is by Andrea Michelli Vicentino and hangs in the doge's palace in Venice.

Venetians in attacking and capturing the city and prepared to stay through the winter.

In January 1203, envoys from Germany had another proposition for the crusaders at Zara. Boniface of Montferrat, an Italian nobleman, had been elected the chief commander of the crusading army. He had visited his cousin, King Philip of Swabia (part of Germany), and the king's Greek wife. The Greek queen's brother—a teen known as Alexius the Younger—was staying there at the time. He had been exiled by his uncle, Alexius III.

The visit couldn't have come at a better time for Alexius the Younger or a worse time for Constantinople. Alexius the Younger convinced Boniface that he would pay the Venetians what the crusaders owed, if the crusaders would detour to Constantinople on their way from Zara to Egypt and help him take the throne from his uncle.

The German envoys brought Alexius the Younger's proposition to the crusading army at Zara. The envoys are reported to have said: "Because you march for God, and for right, and for justice, you must return the inheritance to those who have been despoiled of it, if you are able."

Most of the crusaders did not want to go to Constantinople. The pope in Rome protested against going as well. But Alexius the Younger promised great wealth for little effort—only a show of force. The noblemen, Alexius the Younger, and bishops traveling with the crusaders were said to have fallen on their knees in front of the army, begging for the chance to restore Alexius the Younger to his rightful place.

In May 1203, the crusader fleet set sail for Constantinople. The crusaders and the Venetians that accompanied them expected a popular uprising that would restore the young Alexius the Younger to the throne. But no one seemed to make a move against the current emperor.

In July Alexius the Younger sailed along the city walls and urged his people to support him. Instead, they laughed or threw stones at him. Most seemed to think that it wasn't worth another civil war, or they were angry that Alexius the Younger brought foreign troops to their shores. The Greeks of Byzantium began to fight with the Catholic Europeans (Latins) living in their midst. As the conflict increased, the crusaders captured the settlement of Galata/Pera, moved the massive chain that blocked the Golden Horn, and sailed into the harbor.

The crusaders attacked Constantinople from Galata/Pera and set fire to houses near the wall closest to the harbor. The fire spread, devastating about 125 acres (50 hectares) of the city. Rather than rallying his people, Emperor Alexius III fled west to Adrianople (present-day Edirne) with much of the imperial treasury. Isaac II returned to the throne, but the crusaders kept his son Alexius the Younger until Isaac agreed to fulfill his son's promise to pay the crusaders' debt to the Venetians.

Isaac obliged and the gates were opened to welcome Alexius the Younger and the crusader leaders. Alexius the Younger became joint emperor with his father. The crusader army retreated from the city and waited. The treaty with the Venetians for the warships, men, and supplies would expire in September. After that, it would be too late in the year to sail for Egypt.

But once again, since Alexius III had run off with the

treasury, there was not enough money to pay Venice and send the fleet on its way. Alexius the Younger promised to renew the treaty with the Venetians so that the crusaders could stay until spring—the next sailing season. The Greeks of Byzantium, he swore, would cover the cost of the crusader's Latin army.

"THEY SMASHED THE HOLY IMAGES"

The uneasy peace between Greeks and Roman Catholic crusaders didn't last long. On August 19, 1203, a group of Latins attacked a mosque in Constantinople that had been built when Saladin ruled much of the Middle East. Winds turned the blaze into one of the world's most destructive fires. At least one hundred thousand people were left homeless as fire raged through another 450 acres (180 hectares) of the city. Hagia Sophia barely survived.

The Greeks, many of them forced by the fire to live in tent villages within the city walls, blamed the new emperor for bringing the crusaders to Byzantium. Their Latin neighbors fled the city as new riots broke out between Greeks and Latins. Alexius the Younger was caught between the crusaders, who wanted their reward for putting him in power, and his people, who wanted revenge. He came to rely on an anti-Latin Greek leader named Alexius Ducas, whose black, bushy eyebrows earned him the nickname Mourtzouphlos (roughly meaning "dark-faced" or "gloomy").

In November crusader envoys came to the palace and demanded payment by March 1204 so that the army could continue its journey. Before the emperor could reply, an angry group of Greek officials turned them away. The envoys reported to crusader leaders that Alexius had finally reneged on his promises.

As mob violence threatened to take over the city, the leaders of the crusaders decided to seize property to pay the Venetians for the supplies that Alexius the Younger had promised. They raided the city several times while waiting for sailing season in March. Mourtzouphlos led the defenders of the city, gaining popularity as a new leader. Crowds demanded a new emperor, and a man named Canabus was crowned. Within a few weeks, Mourtzouphlos managed to have Canabus beheaded, Alexius the Younger imprisoned, and himself crowned emperor. Alexius the Younger's elderly father Isaac died.

Mourtzouphlos then strangled Alexius the Younger, though he claimed the teen died of natural causes. This gave the crusader leaders the justification they sought to attack fellow Christians. Mourtzouphlos, they claimed, was a murderer and had no right to rule. They signed a new contract with the Venetians to divide the booty they planned to get from Constantinople when they attacked it in spring. Then they decided how best to govern the city.

On April 8, 1204, the crusaders attacked the walls of Constantinople from their two hundred or so new Venetian war vessels. Their battle cry was "Holy Sepulcher [the tomb in which Jesus was buried]!" The Greeks of Constantinople responded with a battle cry of their own: "Jesus Christ conquers!"

Constantinople had only about twenty decaying ships, but the city's walls were strong, and the defenders outnumbered the

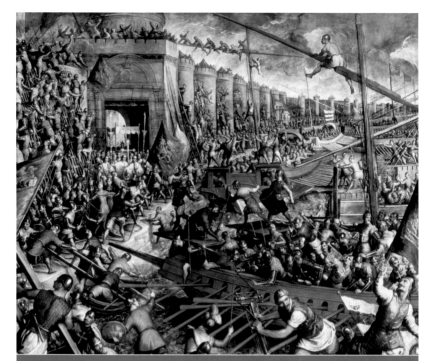

This scene of the 1204 capture of Constantinople by the crusaders was painted by Palma Giovane at the turn of the sixteenth century. It hangs in the doge's palace in Venice.

attackers. The crusaders failed to break through to the city. According to one historian, "As the ships pulled away from the shore the Greeks on the walls hooted and jeered at the defeated attackers. Some of them let down their clouts [pants] and showed their bare buttocks in derision of the fleeting foe."

The crusaders tried again on April 12. This time they found a small gate in the wall that had been sealed shut. While the defenders rained stones, boiling tar, and Greek fire on them, a few knights managed to pry open the gate. They rushed toward the defenders who—quite unexpectedly—fled. More crusaders entered into the city, and they met little resistance.

For centuries no foreign army had successfully breached the walls of Constantinople. The city's people didn't know what to expect. Many thought that the crusaders would simply attack the palace and install a new emperor.

Mourtzouphlos deserted the city, and the remaining government officials chose a new emperor, Constantine Lascaris. The crusader army camped near the seawall waiting for a counterattack that never came.

By dawn the next day, the new emperor and his brother had rowed across the Bosporus to Nicaea, and the palace guards had returned to their barracks to await orders. The Greeks put on their best clothes and lined the streets to greet the new Latin leaders. They were easy targets for the crusader army, which went on a three-day rampage.

The attackers spared no one and nothing, not even Hagia Sophia. One witness described the ransacking of the magnificent church this way: "They smashed the holy images and hurled the sacred relics . . . into places I am ashamed to mention. . . . And they brought horses and mules into the Church, the better to carry off the holy vessels, and the pulpit, and the doors. . . . [N]or was there mercy shown to virtuous matrons, innocent maids or even virgins consecrated to God."

Even though there was little money in the imperial treasury, the Latins found more than enough booty to pay the Venetians for supplying ships and men for the Fourth Crusade. The crusaders melted down hundreds of bronze statues to turn them into coins. Dandolo saved four huge gilded bronze horses from the Hippodrome and shipped them to Venice.

STATUES ON THE MOVE

According to tradition, Greek artisans cast four bronze horses around 400 B.C.—the time of Alexander the Great—and the statues were brought to Rome by the Roman emperor Nero (A.D. 37–68). Later, they stood by the emperor's box at the Hippodrome in Constantinople.

When crusaders sacked Constantinople in 1204, these horses— already about fifteen hundred years old—were sent back to Venice as partial payment to Venice for financing the crusade. The four horses stood over the entrance to Saint Mark's Cathedral in Venice until 1797. In that year, Emperor Napoleon of France conquered Italy and took the bronze horses to Paris. After Napoleon was overthrown in 1815, the horses were returned to Venice. Because of deterioration from air pollution after more than two thousand years of exposure, the original horses (below) were moved to a special exhibit hall in the 1990s. The horses on top of Saint Mark's Cathedral are fiberglass replicas.

Crusader leaders elected Baldwin of Flanders emperor of Byzantium. He was crowned on May 16 in what was left of Hagia Sophia. Few in his army ever made it to the Middle East to fight the Muslims. The Fourth Crusade had turned from a holy war against the rulers of Jerusalem into a rampage against one of the world's greatest Christian cities.

LANGUISHING UNDER THE LATINS AND THE MONGOLS

Baldwin of Flanders and later Latin rulers did little to rebuild Constantinople. The Latin rulers of Constantinople wanted to destroy the Empire of Nicaea—the new state that the Greeks of Constantinople had established in Anatolia soon after the Fourth Crusade. The Greeks concluded a military alliance with the Seljuk Turks, and the tiny new empire managed to survive. It even gained formal recognition by the crusaders.

Meanwhile, a new army of invaders was sweeping down from the steppes (treeless plains) of central Asia and overrunning Anatolia. Genghis Khan had taken the Mongol throne in 1206, shortly after the Fourth Crusade, and was determined to expand his empire. Unlike the Seljuks, who had converted to Islam as they expanded their territory, the Mongols retained the shamanistic beliefs that were the traditional religion of the steppe peoples. They brought devastation along with them, killing millions of people and destroying roads, bridges, irrigation projects, cities, and towns.

Genghis Khan died in 1227, but his son Ogedei Khan continued with his father's plans. The Mongols established a

THEY PLEDGED ALLEGIANCE

The English word *vassal* comes from a Celtic word meaning "servant." During Europe's Middle Ages (about A.D. 500–1500), a vassal was a person who owned land and gave money, men, and supplies to an overlord in exchange for protection. Vassalage also applied to entire cities or regions. Conquerors such as the Romans, Byzantines, or Ottomans often allowed rulers of territories they controlled to remain in power over their own peoples. These vassal kings and princes paid tribute to their conquerors—gold, jewels, and silver—and supplied men and arms in case of war.

vassal system, in which local populations were allowed to continue their way of life so long as they paid 10 percent of their wealth in taxes to the khan (ruler). The Seljuks fell under vassalage to the Mongols, who conquered Baghdad in 1258 and further split the leadership of the Muslim world. They soon ruled an enormous empire stretching from Manchuria across Asia into Europe as far as Hungary and then into the Middle East.

The Greeks in Anatolia still dreamed of wresting Constantinople from the Latins. They considered Michael VIII Palaeologus, a nobleman living near Nicaea, to be the rightful heir to the throne in Constantinople, and they supported his plans to retake the city. Michael VIII worked out an agreement with officials of the city-state of Genoa to use their fleet to attack Venetian forces holding Constantinople. In return, the Genoese would be given special trade arrangements. All Venetian property in Constantinople and elsewhere in the Byzantine Empire would be turned over to them. The Genoese settled in Galata/Pera. They took control of many ports on the Black Sea. But the capture of Constantinople didn't involve the Genoese navy at all.

In the summer of 1261, a Byzantine general and his small army of troops were on their way to test the Latin defenses in Thrace, a former Byzantine region on the western border of Constantinople. In Selymbria (present-day Silivri, Turkey), the general learned that most of the Latin soldiers were out of the city fighting elsewhere and that one of the smaller gates to Constantinople had been left unguarded.

Not wanting to miss this opportunity, the general ordered a handful of men to slip inside the city and open a main gate. The rest of the army entered the city through the main gate. King Baldwin fled, as did the thousand or so Latin inhabitants of the city. The general set fire to the Venetian section of the city, but there was little bloodshed. Within hours the city belonged to the Greeks once again.

A NEW BYZANTIUM AND A NEW THREAT

Emperor Michael VIII returned to Constantinople and tried to bring the dying empire back to life. By 1261 Constantinople was near ruin and the treasury was virtually empty. The emperor made trade and military agreements with Genoa, and in 1267, he gave to the Genoese the

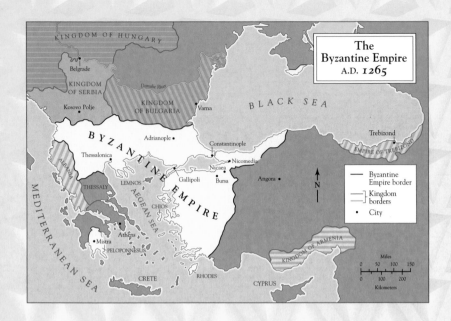

The
Byzantine Empire
A.D. 1265

KINGDOM OF HUNGARY

Belgrade

KINGDOM
OF SERBIA

Kosovo Polje

Danube River

KINGDOM
OF BULGARIA

Varna

BLACK SEA

Trebizond

EMPIRE OF TREBIZOND

Adrianople

Constantinople

Thessalonica

Nicomedia

Nicaea

ALBANIA

THESSALY

LEMNOS

Gallipoli

Bursa

Angora

Byzantine
Empire border

Kingdom
borders

City

N

AEGEAN SEA

CHIOS

MEDITERRANEAN SEA

Mistra

Athens

PELOPONNESUS

CRETE

RHODES

CYPRUS

KINGDOM OF ARMENIA

Miles

0 50 100 150

0 100 200

Kilometers

property rights to the entire district of Galata/Pera, across
the Golden Horn. Without the grain fields and other
resources of Anatolia still held by local Turkish vassals to
the Mongols, Constantinople was forced to depend on foreign merchants and mercenaries. Trebizond, a wealthy city-
state in Anatolia, was still part of Greek Byzantium. But
Trebizond had its own emperor who operated independently
of Constantinople and was little help to the city.

European powers controlled much of the former Byzantine
Empire west of the Bosporus. Heavy taxes, struggles for power
among royal families, religious conflicts, and bouts of the plague
that periodically raged through the area made matters worse.

Once a great sea power, Byzantium no longer had a fleet,
because it cost too much to maintain one. Genoa and
Venice controlled most of the Aegean Sea and fought with

each other over territory and trade rights. Constantinople became a battleground between them. In 1299 Genoa and Venice signed a peace treaty. Three years later, Venetians sailed into the Golden Horn and set fire to nearby buildings. With only a small, poorly equipped army, Byzantine emperor Andronicus II Palaeologus was forced to sign a treaty that gave the Venetians special trading privileges for ten years.

To many Greeks, the Fourth Crusade had made reconciliation between the Orthodox and Roman Catholic Churches impossible. When church leaders met in Constantinople in 1285 to discuss Christian doctrine, the populace refused to change their beliefs or practices. One group thought that it would be better for the survival of Greek Orthodoxy for Constantinople to be ruled by Muslims than to fully submit to the pope in Rome. "Better the Sultan's turban," they said, "than the cardinal's hat."

The Mongols, more interested in booty than in establishing permanent settlements in much of their empire, helped to make that slogan come true. One of the groups caught in the Mongol invasion was the Kayi people, a Turkish tribe that had fled farther and farther into Anatolia, with the Mongols at their heels. According to legend, Kayi horsemen and their leader Tugrul (or Ertugrul) saved a Seljuk ruler and his bodyguards from an attack by Mongols. In gratitude, the Seljuks gave the Kayi a small strip of land west of Konya, near the border with Byzantium. Although the Mongols later defeated the Seljuks in Anatolia, the Kayi were left in relative peace. Their leader was Osman, who took power in 1281. His tribe later became known as the Osmanli—the Ottomans.

CHAPTER THREE

OTTOMANS ON THE RISE

And he gathered up his forces, had them

Take with him the saving bread and wine.

As soon as Lazarus has given out

His orders, then across the level plain

Of Kosovo pour all the Turks.

—from "The Downfall of the Kingdom of Serbia,"
a traditional Slavic poem commemorating
the Battle of Kosovo Polje in 1389

Andronicus II, the emperor of a weakened Greek-ruled Constantinople, saw that Osman and his people were growing stronger and looking to expand westward into Christian Byzantium. In 1303 the emperor resorted to the services of Roger de Flor, the leader of a group of mercenaries called the Grand Company of Catalans (from present-day northern Spain). De Flor offered the use of his men for nine months to rid the emperor of Osman's forces in exchange for money

Roger de Flor (raising his hat) *led his Grand Company of Catalans into Constantinople in 1303. The entrance of the Grand Company was painted by Spaniard José Moreno Carbonero in 1888.*

and the emperor's young niece in marriage. Andronicus II agreed, and the Catalan Company, along with their families (about seven thousand in all), sailed into Constantinople.

The Catalan Company quickly stopped Osman's army from gaining more territory. Over the next two years, they took most of Anatolia from other Turkish leaders. They also took over part of Thrace and had a stronghold in Kallipolis (later called Gallipoli, or Gelibolu). This is a city on the European coast of the Dardanelles, at the tip of the peninsula where the Aegean Sea meets the Sea of Marmara.

Andronicus II rewarded de Flor and another Catalan commander with high positions in his government, but he did not have enough money to pay the troops. The Catalans

HAVE SWORD, WILL TRAVEL

In 1275, when he was eight years old, a German boy named Rutger von Blum was sent to sea on a ship belonging to the Knights Templar. The Templars were a military order of Christian monks who vowed to keep Jerusalem safe from Muslim control. Rutger became a knight, changed his name to its French version, Roger de Flor, and later grew rich from conflicts in the Middle East. After the pope denounced him as a thief, de Flor fled to Genoa, became a pirate, and later fought in a war for control of Sicily. The war over Sicily ended around 1302, leaving thousands of mercenaries out of work. De Flor formed them into the Catalan Company (many of the men were from Catalonia, an area near the Pyrenees Mountains) and offered its services to fight the Turks.

threatened to attack the city. The emperor averted an attack by promising the Catalans all the Byzantine-controlled parts of Anatolia. Roger de Flor and his officers visited Adrianople, a Byzantine city west of Constantinople. De Flor expected that it would soon be his. After drinking and dining with the Byzantine ruler there, the Catalans were attacked by other Byzantine mercenaries and killed.

The remaining Catalans in Anatolia returned to Kallipolis. They joined their main force there and began to capture or destroy many of the towns in Thrace. In 1311 they attacked and captured the city-state of Athens, the capital of present-day Greece. Constantinople was left in an even worse position than it had been before the Catalans arrived.

What little was left of the Byzantine Empire also suffered from civil war. Emperor Andronicus II and his grandson, who would become Andronicus III, vied for power. The battles, which were minor, took place mostly in Thrace. But the turmoil they caused disrupted trade and farming, both vital to the welfare of Constantinople. Other kingdoms, particularly Serbia, gained former Byzantine-controlled territory in the Balkan Peninsula.

Power also changed hands just across the Bosporus in the region that Osman controlled. Breaking with the tradition that allowed for several heirs, Osman determined that only one son would inherit his land and power. That son was Orhan.

Like his father, Orhan was an excellent military leader and a wise statesman. He had honed his skills fighting the Catalans in Anatolia. He waged war when it was

Orhan became the only heir to his father's empire in Anatolia. This watercolor portrait of Orhan was one of A Series of Portraits of the Emperors of Turkey *by Englishman John Young in 1808.*

to his advantage to do so, but he used treaties and other political means to increase his power when possible.

In 1326 the city of Proussa (present-day Bursa) surrendered to the Ottomans after a seven-year siege. Orhan and his followers made this their capital city. From there they could establish a permanent force in the region and consolidate their power. Christians and Muslims alike forged alliances with the Ottomans, who were relatively tolerant of local customs and practices. The Ottomans offered those who fought under their leadership a chance to gain booty and slaves, as well as using it as a means to spread Islam. An alliance with Orhan and his followers was particularly prized because Ottoman territory abutted Christian Byzantium and the relatively wealthy city of Constantinople.

With Proussa under his domain, Orhan set out to lay siege to nearby Nicaea. By then Andronicus III Palaeologus had finally defeated his grandfather. He took the throne and began his attempt to regain a portion of the former Byzantine Empire. In 1329 Andronicus III and his commander-in-chief John VI Cantacuzenus crossed into Anatolia with an army of about four thousand soldiers ready to do battle near Nicaea. Orhan's army had set up camp in a nearby village and prepared to bring the city under siege. The battle for Nicaea was the first time that a Byzantine emperor encountered an Ottoman sultan.

Overwhelmed by Orhan's forces, the Byzantine army retreated to Constantinople. The Ottoman Turks took Nicaea two years later and took Nicomedia six years after that. Skilled in diplomacy as well as military tactics, Ottoman leaders continued to practice traditional crafts such as bow making or leatherworking as part of their nomadic traditions and as a way to gain the allegiance of craft guilds in the region.

AN INVITATION INTO EUROPE

As their territory stretched closer to the Sea of Marmara, separating Europe and Asia, the Ottomans looked to Europe as their next area of expansion. Though originally a landlocked tribe, the Ottomans built up their naval power and began attacking ports on the European side of the Sea of Marmara.

In 1333 Andronicus III and Orhan met again, this time in secret. The emperor agreed to pay the sultan an annual tribute if the Ottomans did not attack the few remaining pieces of the Byzantine Empire in Anatolia. Orhan agreed. He had designs on Europe, not just Anatolia, though he allowed Christians to remain unharmed within his growing empire.

Andronicus III was also intent on building his fleet. Having made peace with the Ottomans, the emperor looked to regain lost territory elsewhere. He hoped to wrest control of islands in the eastern Mediterranean Sea from the city-state of Genoa. He and his commander, John VI Cantacuzenus, also hoped to bring economic and political stability to Constantinople.

It was not to be. Andronicus III died in 1341, leaving behind young children and no coemperor to take over the throne. John VI Cantacuzenus took the reins of power and announced that the rightful emperor was Andronicus's eldest son, nine-year-old John V Palaeologus. The patriarch of the Orthodox Church, the empress mother, and another government official challenged Cantacuzenus for the throne, and civil war erupted once again.

Needing support to maintain his power, John VI Cantacuzenus contacted Orhan. The two men developed a friendship, and in 1346, Cantacuzenus's daughter Theodora married Orhan. She was allowed to keep her Christian faith and to help other Christians living in Orhan's expanding empire.

Meanwhile, the Ottoman Turks continued their efforts to gain a foothold in Europe. Had the rulers in Constantinople, the Balkan kingdoms (especially Serbia and Bulgaria), and the Italian city-states (especially Genoa and Venice) united against the Ottomans at this time, they might have stopped them. Instead, these rulers more often fought among themselves for territory and power.

Religious differences strengthened political and economic rivalries among the Europeans. The administrative structure of the Orthodox Church was based on local autonomy. The bishops or patriarchs of Orthodox Churches in Russia, Serbia, and elsewhere often acted independently of the religious leaders in Constantinople. This differed from the hierarchical Roman Catholic or Latin Church, where all congregations followed the word of the pope. The Orthodox Church continued separate from and sometimes antagonistic toward the pope and the doctrines of the Latin Church.

In 1347 the Black Death (probably bubonic plague) raged through Asia and Europe, and at least one-third of

Byzantium's population died. Between warfare and disease, the empire now included only Thrace, some islands in the northern part of the Aegean Sea, the region around the city of Thessalonica at the northwestern end of the Aegean, and a few areas bordering the southwestern part of the Aegean.

As the battle between rival leaders in Constantinople spread, Cantacuzenus and his men ferried Orhan's soldiers into Europe to fight against his rival's forces—who were also his own Christian subjects. Many Ottomans stayed. Given a foothold in Europe by a Byzantine leader, the Ottoman Turks were in a better position to attack Constantinople from both east and west.

In 1354 a large earthquake hit much of Thrace, leveling hundreds of towns. Suleyman, Orhan's son and general of the Ottoman army, arrived in Thrace with as many Turkish families as he could muster. Many settled in the ruined city of Kallipolis. Soon Kallipolis was overwhelmingly Turkish instead of Greek, and the Ottomans moved farther north and westward into central Europe.

Although Ottoman leaders lived in cities established under the Byzantine and Seljuk empires, most of their people lived in the countryside. No longer nomads, they farmed land, worked at crafts, and paid taxes. Where possible, their houses had private areas or a separate room for women and children. Prosperous farmers might have a walled compound of several buildings. Wives in the wealthiest families remained secluded for much of the day. Their slaves did the shopping and household chores. Ottoman homes at that time had few pieces of furniture. People sat on the floors, which were covered with carpets.

SELJUK CARPETS

During his travels to China, Italian (Genoese) explorer Marco Polo (1254–1324) praised the beauty and quality of the carpets he saw in Anatolia. The peoples of Persia had mastered the arts of carpet weaving centuries before Marco Polo's travels, but the carpets he saw might have been what we call Seljuk carpets. Seljuk women were particularly skillful at using Turkish (or Ghiorde) knots, a special weaving technique. The Seljuk Turks greatly influenced Persian carpet making, even after the Mongols destroyed much of the Seljuk Empire. Turkish knots are still used in carpet making in some regions of the Middle East and Asia.

From about the age of seven, boys attended school to study Islam and other subjects, including science, music, and poetry. Girls stayed home and learned how to run a household. Girls also studied basic prayers and learned to read and write. By the time a girl was twelve or thirteen, she was married off to someone her father selected. She then became a part of her husband's household.

OTTOMANS INTO SERBIA

Civil war between the Palaeologus and Cantacuzenus families drained the resources from Constantinople, which was fast becoming surrounded by Turkish territory. Serbia's ruler, Stefan Dusan, died in 1355, and his death dissolved united rule over much of the Balkan area. This left a power vacuum that the Ottomans were soon able to exploit. If a Christian town did not resist capture, it could keep its churches and operate with some independence. The taxes that the Ottomans levied were often less than those the townspeople had to pay to the Byzantine emperor.

When Suleyman died, Orhan chose another son, Murad, to be his successor. Murad's mother was John Cantacuzenus's daughter Theodora. Ottoman leaders could have up to four wives according to Moslem laws, as well as a number of consorts. They expected that sons would have different mothers. Each mother could concentrate her efforts on her favorite son in hopes that he would be deemed the most capable successor.

Murad, who became sultan in 1361 (a year before his father's death), consolidated and then expanded his father's empire. He moved the Ottoman capital from Bursa in Asia to Adrianople in Europe. He no longer depended on men who fought for any leader who could bring them the benefits of war— more slaves and greater wealth. Instead, Murad

Murad expanded the Ottoman Empire and moved the capital to Adrianople in Europe in the mid-fourteenth century. This portait is from a sixteenth-century Italian manuscript.

The janissary was a fighting force made up of Ottoman prisoners of war. It grew to be feared in battle. This drawing of a janissary archer is from 1300.

reorganized his army into two main groups that would owe their allegiance to him as sultan.

The first group was the regular army, or militia. This was made up of men who rented land from the sultan in exchange for military service when called. The second was known as the *yeniceri* (new soldier), or janissary, who served the sultan for life. The first janissaries were prisoners of war. The sultan enslaved them but paid them for their services.

By the time Murad took power, civil war in Byzantium had ended— at least for the moment. John VI Cantacuzenus retired to a monastery, the home of a religious order, and John V Palaeologus became emperor. Seeing the Ottoman threat to Constantinople, John V left his empire in the hands of his son Andronicus and traveled with two other sons to Hungary and then to Italy to ask for aid and to hire mercenaries. This trip in 1366 marked the first time that a Byzantine emperor had left Constantinople to seek help from Christian rulers in the West. Byzantium's leaders would continue to make trips west for the next century—often in vain.

John V returned home virtually empty handed. To make matters worse, Bulgaria's rulers briefly detained the emperor at the border between Bulgaria and Hungary. Even so, John V set out on another trip soon afterward. In 1369 he personally submitted to the authority of the pope in Rome, forsaking his ties to Orthodox Christianity in the hopes of getting aid from the Latin Christians of western Europe. On that trip, he was arrested by authorities in Venice as a debtor. Through the help of his son, Manuel, John was released and returned home in 1371 with nothing to show for his efforts.

Also in 1369, the Ottomans defeated a Serbian army sent to stop their advance into the southern Balkans. Thrace, southern Bulgaria, and much of Macedonia were now clearly controlled by the Ottomans. What was left of Byzantium became a vassal state to the Ottoman Turks, paying a yearly tribute and supplying military aid. The vassalage system allowed local rulers to retain some of their power and gave the Ottomans the ability to control a large region without maintaining a large army there.

Vassalage required obedience that sometimes came at a high price. As part of his agreement with Murad, John V and his men joined forces with the Ottomans against a group of Seljuk Turks who still controlled some territory in Anatolia. Andronicus, John V's son, who governed Byzantium in his father's absence, joined with Murad's son to revolt against both their fathers. Murad crushed the rebellion. He blinded his son and ordered John V to blind

Andronicus. John V obeyed but injured his son in such a way that Andronicus kept some of his sight. Andronicus was imprisoned in Constantinople, and his brother Manuel became coemperor with John V.

The quest for power meant ever-shifting alliances. A few years later, the Venetians engineered Andronicus's escape from prison. Andronicus promised to help Murad consolidate his territory in Thrace, and Murad gave Andronicus enough soldiers to seize the throne from John V and Manuel and imprison them.

Three years later, John V and Manuel escaped, and they too sought aid from the Ottoman sultan. They promised more money and more armed forces. Murad agreed to help. Meanwhile, the Venetians decided that Andronicus had not been a reliable and effective ally. They teamed up with the Ottomans and helped to reinstall John V and Manuel as coemperors of Byzantium.

In 1389 Serbia tried to assert independence from the Ottomans. Serbian and Ottoman armies clashed at the Battle of Kosovo Polje—"the field of blackbirds." A Serb posing as a deserter—possibly the son of the Serbian prince Lazar—was ushered into Murad's tent. Instead of revealing information about the Serbian troops, he stabbed the sultan to death. The Serb assassin was immediately killed, and Murad's son Bayezid quickly took command. The Ottoman troops did not hear of the sultan's death until the battle was over—a battle that the Ottomans barely won. Prince Lazar also died in this battle. The Battle of Kosovo Polje became the subject of songs and stories for centuries to come.

This illustration shows a Serb killing Ottoman sultan Murad in the Battle of Kosovo Polje. He was actually stabbed while in his tent by a Serb who gained entrance claiming to be a spy.

IMPERIAL POWER

As the new Ottoman ruler, Bayezid soon conquered all the Balkans. Bayezid was called Yildirim (thunderbolt). Some said the name showed how quickly he moved his troops during war. Others said it referred to the sultan's quick temper.

Bayezid expanded the janissary corps by *devshirme* (gathering). The Ottomans took boys as hostages from Christian families in conquered areas and educated them for service to the sultan. Many of the boys became janissaries. Where possible, Bayezid used Christian Serb janissaries to fight in Muslim-held parts of Anatolia and Muslim Turks to fight in Christian-held parts of Europe.

CAMELS

The camels of Anatolia carried the fate of an empire on their backs. Bred to endure a cold, wet climate, a camel could transport about 550 pounds (250 kg) of an army's equipment and supplies over harsh terrain—about twice as much as a horse or mule could carry.

Camels enabled Bayezid's army to travel swiftly to battlegrounds from the Euphrates River to the Danube River. After conquering the Mediterranean port of Antalya in 1399, Bayezid claimed ten thousand camels as part of his booty. Camels remained the key to transportation in Turkey until the twentieth century, when railroads displaced them.

Bayezid's government was as strong as its military. While the traditional Turkish nomads were loyal to a particular leader, the Ottoman system emphasized loyalty to an office. The sultan was obeyed because he was the sultan. This new state bureaucracy was needed to collect the taxes to supply a vast army and bring prosperity to the empire.

By the end of the fourteenth century, the Ottomans had transformed themselves from a small tribe of Asian nomads into an imperial power based on farmers, city dwellers, tradespeople, government workers, and a standing army.

With territories in the Balkans and Anatolia under control, Bayezid began to make his final plans to capture Constantinople. He sent a gift-laden ambassador to Cairo,

Egypt, with a request for the caliph. Through his ambassador, Bayezid described himself as a simple *beg* (or bey), meaning "prince" or "chief." Since he and his family had conquered so much of the territory that had belonged to Rome, Bayezid asked the caliph for a diploma that gave him the official title Sultan of Rum. The caliph granted his request, and in 1395, the new sultan began his blockade of Constantinople.

Bayezid (center), shown in this 1380 engraving, strengthened the Ottoman army and government. He then laid plans to conquer Constantinople.

A CHAPTER FOUR
A MATTER OF TIME

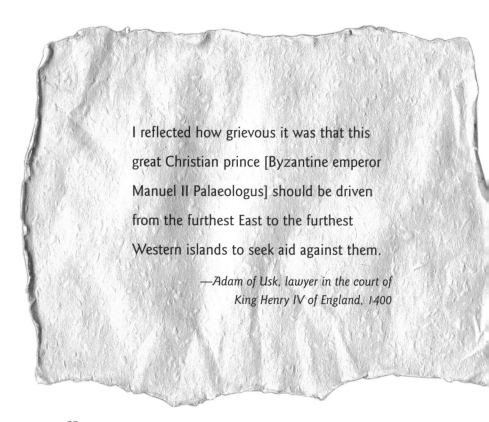

I reflected how grievous it was that this
great Christian prince [Byzantine emperor
Manuel II Palaeologus] should be driven
from the furthest East to the furthest
Western islands to seek aid against them.

—*Adam of Usk, lawyer in the court of
King Henry IV of England, 1400*

Bayezid planned to breach Constantinople's massive walls or
starve the city's population into surrender. He pulled part of
his army from the Balkans and marched them to
Constantinople. Byzantine emperor Manuel II Palaeologus
(his father John V had died a few years earlier) appealed to
Christian rulers in Europe for help. So, too, did the two rival
Roman popes at that time (one in Rome and one in Avignon,
France), who called for a crusade against the Ottomans.

Over one hundred thousand men from Poland, Germany, France, Italy, and elsewhere joined under the leadership of the king of Hungary to launch the crusade. In 1396 they reached the Bulgarian city of Nicopolis. Bayezid took most of his army there and defeated the crusaders.

Then it was back to Constantinople. In 1397 the people there watched in horror as the Ottomans built the castle known as Anadolu Hisar (meaning "Anatolia fortress") on the Asian side of the Bosporus, right across from their city. Bayezid the Thunderbolt was getting ready to strike.

A French military leader named Marechal Boucicaut arrived in Constantinople in 1399 with twelve hundred soldiers and money from the king of France. He quickly realized that much more aid was needed. Fewer than one hundred thousand people

In 1396 the Ottoman army of Bayezid defeated the makings of a new crusade led by the king of Hungary. This watercolor was painted by an Ottoman artist in the sixteenth century.

lived in Constantinople, though the area had held more than one million people two hundred years earlier. The crowded metropolis that had once seemed hemmed in by the city's massive walls was reduced to villages or districts with vast areas of open space in between. The Venetians had a thriving district near the harbor, but the main street of Constantinople held only a few shops and houses. The old Imperial Palace stood abandoned, the lead from its roof stripped and sold. The Cathedral of Holy Apostles badly needed repair. Even the once-splendid Hagia Sophia had suffered through earthquakes and had begun to decay. It seemed that Constantinople would soon fall to either Latin Christian or Muslim forces. It was only a matter of time. Boucicaut convinced the emperor to plead personally for more support from King Charles of France and anyone else in Europe who might listen.

In the spring of 1400, Manuel II Palaeologus left his nephew in charge of

Manuel II Palaeologus traveled through Europe seeking military support from European rulers to help protect Constantinople from the Ottomans. This portrait is from a fifteenth-century French manuscript.

MALEDICTA

Maledicta are words of evil intent. They often make one group of people feel superior to another group of people. Each side calls the other "unbelievers" or "infidels" and accuses the other of atrocious acts. Both Muslim and Christian leaders have used maledicta to encourage their followers to fight holy wars.

the empire and sailed with a few ministers to Venice. As he traveled through northern Italy to France, he received many honors but little support. In June he arrived in Paris, where King Charles had arranged an elegant reception in the palace that later became the Louvre museum.

Finding that no one on the mainland of European would help, the emperor and his ministers traveled to England. On Christmas Day 1400, King Henry IV gave a banquet for them. Those at the banquet remembered the "emperor of the Greeks," as they called him, wearing spotless white robes and carrying himself with dignity. The white clothing meant that the emperor was in deep mourning. Henry IV promised military aid. He presented Manuel II with money donated in church collection boxes for the purpose of saving Byzantium from the "unbelievers."

Manuel II returned to Paris a few weeks later. He stayed there for a year, trying to garner aid for his besieged city. Then in September 1402, an envoy from Constantinople arrived with amazing news. The siege of Constantinople had been lifted.

TATARS

Earlier that year, the great Tatar warrior Timur (meaning "iron") had attacked Ottoman territory in Anatolia. Historical records also refer to Timur as Timur-i-lenk, or Timur the Lame. He is known in English stories as Tamerlane, or Tamburlane. The Tatars were part of the Mongol confederation from central Asia. Claiming to be descended from Genghis Khan, Timur had already conquered Persia and parts of Russia and India.

Bayezid temporarily lifted the siege of Constantinople to move most of his army into Anatolia and defend his territory against the Tatar invasion. The Ottomans and Tatars clashed near Ankara in July 1402. Timur captured Bayezid and his son Musa and defeated the Ottoman army. He sacked Anatolia and then returned to his home base in Samarkand (an ancient city in present-day Uzbekistan). Timur's interests lay to the east in China rather than in Europe.

Bayezid and his son were captured by the Tatars in 1402. They and members of their army were led, hands bound, before Timur in this Turkish painting from 1600.

Although treated relatively well, Bayezid died in captivity. Musa was set free to bury him in the old Ottoman capital of Bursa. Timur returned Ottoman lands in Anatolia to various Seljuk and other Turkish princes who had been former vassals of the Ottomans. But he allowed the Ottomans to keep the small portion of land in northwest Anatolia that had been their original territory.

After Timur died in 1405, the Ottoman dynasty struggled to regain its former power. Prince Musa claimed he was the rightful heir. He rallied popular support among the Christian and Muslim peasants and others in the European part of the former Ottoman Empire. Musa regained control of land in Thrace and Serbia, and in 1410, he once again laid siege to Constantinople.

Musa's brother Mehmed claimed he was the rightful heir to the Ottoman sultanate. Promising better relations with his neighbors, Mehmed gained support among the peoples of Anatolia, the rulers of Serbia, and the Byzantine emperor Manuel II Palaeologus. Manuel II thought that Mehmed would keep Byzantium as a vassal state and allow the Greeks to retain control of Constantinople

In 1413 Mehmed captured Musa and strangled him (so as not to shed royal blood). Later, he squashed a revolt of Musa's supporters. After consolidating his power, Mehmed returned several territories to Manuel II, including Thessalonica, a major port in the Balkans. Mehmed died in 1421, and his son Murad II became sultan. Without Mehmed's support, the Byzantines were too weak to hold Thessalonica, and the Venetians gained control of that city in 1423.

FRATRICIDE

Soon after Osman took power, fratricide (killing a brother) became an accepted practice. At about the age of fourteen, Ottoman princes were circumcised as a rite of manhood. Then they were sent to govern parts of the Ottoman Empire. Once the sultan and his advisers determined which prince would make the best ruler, the other princes were killed. They were usually drowned or strangled with a silk cord so as not to shed royal blood.

This practice became part of Ottoman law by the time of Mehmed II, who said: "To whichever of my sons the Sultanate may be vouchsafed [granted], it is proper for him to put his brothers to death, to preserve the order of the world. Most of the *ulema* [religious judges] allow this. Let them therefore act accordingly."

FUELING THE RENAISSANCE

By this time, many Byzantines had fled to Italy from Constantinople and other parts of the empire. Most of them emigrated to Venice from Constantinople, seeking a new and prosperous life safe from Ottoman attack. The wealthiest of the émigrés supported fellow Greeks until they could be established in Italy. A family of Greek shipbuilders dominated the Venetian docks between 1400 and 1442. Others from Byzantium brought with them their skills as tailors, tradespeople, and merchants.

Scholars, theologians, and envoys from the Byzantine emperor often settled in Rome. They carried with them a culture that many educated Italians lacked. This was partly because, for several centuries, secular (not religious) education had been abandoned in Italy. During those centuries, young Byzantines who continued their education past the age of fourteen would have studied the writings of ancient Greek dramatists, historians, philosophers, and poets. These writings, brought to Italy by the Byzantine émigrés, played an importance part in Europe's Renaissance—a period of intellectual "rebirth" from roughly the fourteenth to the sixteenth centuries.

Leonardo Bruni, an Italian historian who died in 1444, once claimed that Byzantine diplomat Manuel Chrysoloras (1350–1415) brought back to the Italians an understanding of classical Greek that had been lost for seven hundred years. Present-day historians agree that Bruni was exagerating. In 1391 Chrysoloras did give lessons in Greek to a

This illustration from an eleventh-century Greek manuscript shows a school of philosophy students in Constantinople. Byzantine scholars fled to Italy during the Ottoman attacks on Constantinople during the 1300s and brought new learning to all of Europe.

Venetian who then arranged for him to teach Greek grammar and literature at the University of Florence. But it was only for three years. Many other Byzantines, both before and after Chrysoloras, influenced Italian art and science. Chrysoloras translated the works of Greek philosophers Plato and Homer into Latin, and his students were among the earliest Renaissance scholars.

THE FINAL YEARS

Manuel II struggled to find aid for Constantinople, but he refused to force his Greek Orthodox people to accept the authority of the Catholic pope in Rome. Manuel's aide, George Sphrantzes, wrote that the emperor warned his son John that "the impious [Muslims] dread the day we come to terms and unite with the Franks [western Europeans]; they believe that if this happens, they will suffer because of us a great misfortune at the hands of the Christians of the West." The emperor feared that the Ottomans would think unity with Rome was the

Murad II became sultan in 1421. In 1444 he swore he would not cross the Danube River and attack Hungary. This portrait of Murad is a nineteenth-century Turkish watercolor.

John VIII Palaeologus traveled to Rome and agreed to a union with the Catholic Church. This 1459 fresco by Benozzo Gozzoli is in a palace chapel in Florence, Italy.

first step in preparing for a united offensive against Muslim-held territories.

Such unity was precisely what his son, the next emperor, John VIII Palaeologus, wanted. He thought that only the pope had the power and authority to rally support in Europe for Constantinople. Shortly after John VIII became emperor in 1425, he opened negotiations with Pope Eugenius IV. The pope invited John VIII to bring a delegation of patriarchs to a synod (council) of leading religious scholars in Italy. John's delegation eventually agreed to a religious union with Rome. Other eastern patriarchs refused to be bound by the delegation's decision, but the pope chose to act as if the churches had reunited. He called for a crusade against the Turks.

Meanwhile, the Ottomans were expanding their territory

> "Lord John . . . departed for the scheduled synod [religious meeting]. Would I that he had never left! . . . [T]he synod was the single most important cause for the attack that the impious [Muslims] launched against our City [Constantinople], which resulted in the siege, our enslavement, and our great misfortunes."
>
> —George Sphrantzes, ca. 1477, about meetings between John VIII Palaeologus and Catholic religious leaders in 1438 and 1439

in Europe. In 1430 they captured Thessalonica from the Venetians. In 1439 they captured a fortress on the Danube River and were threatening Hungary. The Hungarians and their allies—responding to the pope's call for a new crusade—were able to push the Turks back. In June 1444, the opposing sides came to an agreement. Murad II swore on the Quran and King Ladislas of Hungary swore on the Gospels of the Bible that neither army would cross the Danube River to fight the other for ten years. The sultan agreed to move most of his army back to Anatolia.

Then the sultan did what no one had expected: he gave the throne to his son Mehmed II, who was then only twelve years old. Born to a slave girl in Adrianople in 1432, Mehmed II had spent his childhood with his mother and nurse. After the death of Mehmed II's two older half brothers (with nobler mothers), Murad II brought Mehmed II to his court, showed him how to rule, and gave him a thorough education. Mehmed II studied science, philosophy, and Islamic and Greek literature. He learned to speak Greek and possibly other languages.

Perhaps Murad II thought that a ten-year truce would give Mehmed II time to learn how to rule his father's empire. But no sooner had Murad II reached Anatolia, then the news arrived that the Hungarian king had violated the truce and crossed the Danube River into Bulgaria. The pope had absolved King Ladislas of his oath on the grounds that an oath sworn by an infidel such as Murad II was not valid, and he sent the king and his crusaders back into battle.

The Orthodox Christians in Constantinople were dismayed by the pope's behavior, and Emperor John VIII refused to help the Hungarians. In Anatolia, Murad II took back the reins of power. In November 1444, Genoese sailors helped ferry the Ottoman army across to Europe, where they fought crusaders near the Black Sea port of Varna (in present-day Bulgaria), north of Constantinople. The Turks won a decisive victory. King Ladislas died, and only a few Hungarians escaped.

Mehmed II returned to the throne soon afterward, under the guidance of Murad II's trusted grand vizier (chief officer), Candarli Halil Pasha. The boy sultan was well liked by many at court and was considered a genius. Halil, though, didn't approve of Mehmed II's independent ways, his rowdy behavior, and his determination to attack Constantinople. In 1446 the grand vizier persuaded Murad II to take back the throne once again. Obeying his father's order, Mehmed II married the daughter of a Muslim prince from present-day Turkmenistan and went to live in his father's palace in Manisa in Anatolia.

The Hungarians organized yet another crusade, this time meeting the Turks once again in Kosovo in October 1448.

Mehmed II fought alongside his father, who had armed his best soldiers with new weapons that fired bullets using gunpowder. The Turks won.

About two weeks later, John VIII Palaeologus died. His mother, Empress Helena, rallied support for her youngest son, Constantine, to take the throne. Before the coronation, George Sphrantzes visited Murad II. Describing the expert diplomacy required of a vassal state surrounded by the Ottoman's expanding empire, Sphrantzes wrote that he "set out with an embassy to inform the sultan that the empress, the brother, right of birth, and the love and wisdom of nearly the whole population of the City chose Lord Constantine emperor. The sultan approved the choice and sent me away with honor and gifts." To ensure that power passed quickly to the new emperor, the leaders of Byzantium decided to break with a thousand-year tradition of a coronation in Constantinople. Instead, they crowned the new emperor in Mistras, the fortified capital of the Morea region in Greece.

Emperor Constantine XI Palaeologus began his reign in 1449. He gave his two brothers control of Mistras and the rest of Morea and tried to unite the political and religious factions in Constantinople. According to Sphrantzes, the city was in "great need of funds" and required a period of peace.

In February 1451, Halil Pasha announced to Mehmed II that Murad II had died peacefully in Adrianople. The once and future sultan kept Halil as grand vizier but replaced many other ministers in his father's government. He arranged for a younger half brother to be killed and sent his father's Serbian wife, Mara, back to her father's court.

A CAUSE FOR GRIEF

Sphrantzes heard of Murad II's death from the emperor of Trebizond, while on a mission to that Byzantine city-state. The emperor thought Sphrantzes would be delighted. Sphrantzes replied: "Lord, this news . . . is a cause for grief. . . . The late sultan was an old man, had given up the conquest of our City. . . . This man, who just became sultan, is young and an enemy of the Christians since childhood."

Sphrantzes tried to arrange for Constantine XI, a widower, to marry the widowed Serbian princess Mara, who was Christian. He thought it would strengthen alliances and preserve Constantinople. Having spent years as a wife of an Ottoman sultan, Mara refused to remarry.

Many leaders and vassals in Europe and Asia came to Mehmed's court. He treated them in a friendly manner and confirmed his father's treaties, including his father's pledge not to conquer Constantinople.

Many Europeans chose to believe that the young sultan was no threat, but Sphrantzes and Constantine XI sent an ambassador to Rome to once again seek help. The pope responded: "If you, with your nobles and the people of Constantinople, accept the decree of union, you will find Us and Our venerable brother, the Cardinals of the holy Roman Church, ever eager to support your honor and your empire. But if you and your people refuse to accept the decree, you will force Us to take such measures as are necessary for your salvation and Our honour." Again, the pope offered Rome's help only if the Greek Church submitted to Roman Catholic rule.

Less than a year after his father's death, Mehmed II invaded Byzantine territory. He expelled Greeks from their

Rumeli Hisar is a fortress that was built by the Ottomans in 1452 on the western, or European, side of the Bosporus, north of Constantinople.

towns and villages and took their property. He ordered masons and laborers to tear down churches and monasteries on the Asian side of the Bosporus, across from Constantinople, and to collect building materials from the ruins.

Realizing that Mehmed II was preparing another siege, the emperor sent diplomats to plead with him. Mehmed II refused to meet with them. Constantine XI sent a second set of diplomats. This time they were decapitated.

During the summer of 1452, the Turks built the castle called Rumeli Hisar (Roman fortress) on the European (or Roman) side of Bosporus. A Hungarian engineer named Urban offered to make cannons to protect Constantinople. The emperor could not afford to pay Urban's salary, so Urban sold his cannon-making services to the sultan. Cannons had been used in Europe since the fourteenth century, but they were not very reliable. Mehmed II ordered experiments. He was determined to make the cannons work.

RELIGIOUS UNITY AT LAST?

In October 1452, Cardinal Isidore arrived in Constantinople from Rome. The cardinal was Greek and had been a member of the Greek Orthodox Church before taking a leadership position among the Catholics in Rome. At the pope's request—and with the pope's money—he had stopped in Naples and bought the services of two hundred archers to use for the protection of Constantinople. Isidore hoped to enforce the decree of unity that had been signed by Byzantine emperor John VIII years earlier and to bring military aid to Constantinople.

Not everyone in Constantinople thought that religious unity with the West was wise, even if it did bring aid. Some were committed to following their faith no matter what happened. Others thought that Greek culture and Orthodox religious beliefs had a better chance of surviving under Muslim rule.

Mehmed II's plans for Constantinople were proving to be more dangerous than those of his father. The sultan positioned at least one of Urban's cannons at his newly completed castle. He demanded that every ship entering the waters near Constantinople stop at the castle for inspection. The people of Constantinople watched as two Venetian ships defied the order, dodged the cannon fire, and escaped into safe harbor. But about two weeks later, the cannon sank another Venetian ship. The Turks decapitated the surviving crew and impaled the ship's captain.

Soon afterward, Constantine XI and his highest officials attended a service at Hagia Sophia. The decree of religious union with Rome was read aloud. Sphrantzes wrote, "The emperor consented to have the pope's name commemorated in our services, by necessity, as we hoped to receive some aid. Whoever were willing would pronounce the commemoration in Saint Sophia; the rest would incur no blame and remain peaceful. . . ." He continued ruefully, "Six months later we had received as much aid from Rome as had been sent to us by the sultan of Cairo"—meaning nothing.

In fact, Pope Nicholas was trying to gather support in Europe but without much success. Rulers were either unable or unwilling to commit troops to another crusade. Some thought the walls that had protected the great city for so long would still stand. Furthermore, the treasury of Constantinople was practically empty, so not even mercenaries could be bought. The king of Catalonia (in present-day Spain) offered to help if the emperor gave him the Greek island of Lemnos, and the emperor agreed. Genoa did not officially send help. Venice sent out orders to protect Christians but not provoke Turks.

Individual soldiers and crusaders from as far away as Scotland arrived to defend the city from the Muslim Turks. In January 1453, a Genoese military leader named Giovanni Giustiniani Longo came with seven hundred well-armed soldiers. Constantine persuaded Venetian supporters in Constantinople to cooperate with him despite the distrust between Genoa and Venice.

While some came to the city, others fled. Perhaps more would have left then had they known that the sultan had ordered Urban to make a cannon that was twice as large as his earlier ones. The barrel of this monstrous cannon was reported to be 26 feet 8 inches (8 m) long. The cannonballs were said to weigh about 1,300 pounds (591 kg) each. When tested in Adrianople, the cannon hurled a cannonball about a mile (1.8 kilometers), creating a hole about 6 feet (2 m) deep.

The sultan was pleased. He ordered his men to level the road from Adrianople to Constantinople and to strengthen the bridges. In March the monster and the roads were ready. It is reported that seven hundred men were needed to place Urban's cannon on a giant cart. Pulled by sixty oxen and guided by two hundred men, the cart and cannon rolled slowly eastward toward Constantinople. Turkish warships sailed for the Sea of Marmara. Mehmed Fatih (Conqueror) was on his way.

CHAPTER FIVE

1453

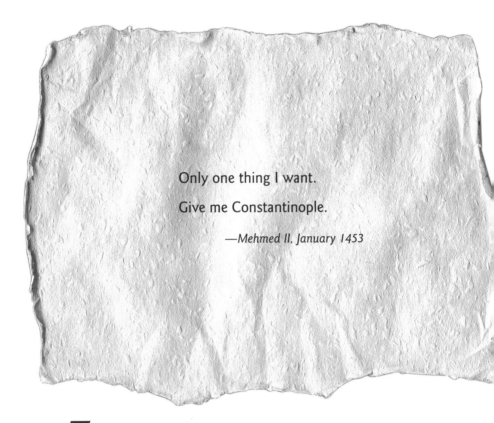

Only one thing I want.

Give me Constantinople.

—*Mehmed II, January 1453*

Torrential rains plagued Constantinople during March 1453, slowing the pace of the attackers and hampering the defenders in the city. Emperor Constantine XI expected Mehmed II and his army to approach the city by land. Throughout the winter, the people of Constantinople had cleared debris from the great moat and strengthened the city walls.

Most of the defenders at Constantinople were Christian, but they also included Muslim Turks led by Prince Orhan, an enemy of the Ottomans. On the other hand, not all the men who fought for Mehmed II were Muslim. Some Christians and Muslims viewed the coming battle as a religious war. Others saw it as a struggle over political and economic power in the region. Many of the mercenary soldiers on both sides saw it as a way to earn a living and to share in the booty that came with victory.

On April 2, the day after Easter Sunday, the people of Constantinople first spied Mehmed II's approaching army. It was time to destroy the bridges spanning the moat and to close the city gates.

A Venetian named Nicolo Barbaro had arrived that spring. A ship's surgeon, he remained in Constantinople when the ship's captain decided to help defend the city. According to Barbaro, who kept a diary of the siege: "All the nobles of Venice [in Constantinople] went to the Emperor, and put to him that he should appoint four captains for the four city gates, that is those on the landward side. Thereupon the Most Serene Emperor answered kindly that Constantinople had come to belong more to the Venetians than to the Greeks, and because he wished the Venetians well, he was willing to give the four gates of the city with all their keys into their charge."

The defenders had built a boom to prevent ships from sailing into the Golden Horn harbor. "It was made of huge round pieces of wood," Barbaro wrote, "joined together with large nails of iron and thick iron links, one end of it being inside the walls of Constantinople, and the other inside the walls of [Galata/Pera]. . . . Seeing that we were so strong at sea, we felt very confident against the fleet of the faithless Turks.

[N]evertheless, the Most Serene Emperor had grave doubts all the while concerning the treacherous Turk his enemy, who was waiting from day to day to join battle with him."

Constantine XI had every reason to worry. The emperor had asked his minister George Sphrantzes to take a secret count of all the able-bodied men in the city. Sphrantzes wrote: "In spite of the great size of our City, our defenders amounted to 4,773 Greeks, as well as just about 200 foreigners." Later estimates show that there were about two thousand foreigners but still only about seven thousand people to protect the city's 14 miles (23 km) of walls.

By April 5, the enemy camp just outside the city walls held over one hundred thousand men. The elite corps of janissaries guarded Mehmed II's red and gold tent. The regular army took up positions in two main areas: to the west of the city along the low-lying area around the Lycus River, which flowed through the middle of Constantinople, and near Galata/Pera on the northern shore of the Golden Horn. The *bashi-bazouks*—an irregular army of mercenaries

More than one hundred thousand Ottoman troops camped outside the walls of Constantinople in April 1453. This scene was painted by the seventeenth-century Corsican artist Micco Spadaro.

and slaves—settled in various camps.

According to Barbaro, the Turks had 145 ships anchored at the Double Columns, a harbor in the Bosporus 2 miles (3 km) north of the city. Most of these ships were low decked and guided by oars.

The emperor had no navy. Alvise Diedo, a Venetian merchant-captain, took charge of defending the Golden Horn harbor. There were an estimated twenty-six ships equipped for fighting and some smaller boats. Nearly all the ships were high decked, without oars, and dependent on sails.

Each side made a show of strength. About one thousand Venetian sailors paraded along the length of the walls. The Turks captured two small neighboring castles—one in Therapia, on a hill overlooking the Bosporus, and the other in Studius, a village near the Sea of Marmara. Mehmed II had about seventy-five prisoners from the castles brought in front of the city walls and impaled. Then, in keeping with Islamic tradition, the sultan offered the citizens of Constantinople a chance to surrender. If they did so, he promised not to harm them or their property. The emperor refused.

THE SIEGE BEGINS

On April 6, opening shots from Turkish cannons damaged a wall near the Charisian Gate about a half mile (0.8 km) north of the Lycus River. Defenders repaired the wall. Mehmed II repositioned his cannons and, a few days later, began bombarding the walls again. Soon an outer wall in the Lycus Valley was destroyed, but the defenders built an earthen and wood stockade to take its place.

"[When Urban's cannon was fired,] the explosion made all the walls of the city shake, and all the ground inside, and even the ships in the harbor felt the vibrations of it. Because of the great noise, many women fainted with the shock which the firing of it gave them.

—Nicolo Barbaro, 1453

Urban's monster and the other cannons took so much preparation to fire that they could be set off only seven times each day. Each firing brought deafening destruction. The leather sheets and bales of wool the Greeks used to fill the breaks that cannonballs left in the walls were no help.

On April 15, four ships laden with supplies for Constantinople sailed into the Sea of Marmara. The pope had paid for three ships from Genoa, and ambassadors from Constantinople had purchased another from Sicily.

As these ships approached, Suleiman Baltoghlu, admiral of the Turkish fleet, set dozens of ships to destroy them. Barbaro wrote that "the water could hardly be seen for the vessels of these evil dogs." Winds blowing against the current made it hard to maneuver, and the oars on the Turkish ships got in the way. The Italian ships were taller and well armed. Their sailors beat back the Turks with javelins, axes, stones, and arrows. The Sicilian ship attacked with Greek fire. Despite the odds, all four ships made it safely inside the boom.

Mehmed II was furious. He threatened to behead Baltoghlu, but sailors testified to their admiral's bravery.

Baltoghlu kept his head but lost his rank and property.

A few nights later, Mehmed II's army was also unsuccessful on land. His soldiers beat drums, clanged cymbals, and shouted battle cries as they rushed toward a stockade. Ottoman archers and javelin throwers attacked the stockade's defenders, while other troops tried to burn the stockade's wood planks and tear it down with hooks attached to their lances. The defenders led by Giovanni Giustiniani fought fiercely. They had better armor and weapons. After four hours, the Ottoman army withdrew.

Bombardments continued. On April 21, the Bactatinian tower fell, along with a large section of wall. Barbaro wrote: "Now . . . everyone considered himself lost. . . . I tell you, that if on this day the Turks had been willing to make an attack on the walls with only ten thousand men . . . they would have succeeded in getting into the city."

Instead, the Turks withdrew. The defenders rushed to fill the breach with wooden beams, vines, branches, earth, and rubble. Still the sultan did not order an attack. He was likely overseeing construction of an extraordinary road that led from the sea over a hillside near Galata/Pera and down into the Golden Horn harbor.

By dawn the next day, about seventy Turkish ships had sailed down toward the boom across the harbor. One by one, they were carefully hoisted onshore. Oxen teams and pulleys dragged the ships onto wooden rollers greased with animal fat. Sailors raised the ships' flags and pretended to row their way along the road. Within hours the ships were safely inside the Golden Horn.

Constantinople's Venetians planned to burn the Turkish

fleet, which threatened 5 miles (8 km) of seawall. Then, according to Barbaro, the Genoese leaders in Galata/Pera found out and offered to help if the Venetians waited a day or two more. Meanwhile, according to Barbaro, these same leaders warned the sultan of the Venetians' plans and the attack failed. Since Barbaro was a Venetian and biased against the Genoese, it is possible that his account of the events is not entirely accurate.

Constantinople's storehouses were running short of the grain that was vital to sustain the population through a siege. Turkish ships in the harbor prevented fishing boats from going out, and there were few sheep and cattle within the city. Desperate to seek aid, twelve volunteers disguised as Turks boarded a Venetian ship on May 3. They hoisted Turkish flags, slipped through the boom, and sailed toward the Aegean Sea.

With half of their fleet inside the harbor, the Turks built a pontoon bridge out of barrels to make it easy to transport men and supplies between Constantinople and Galata/Pera. Mehmed II continued to bombard the city and attack the walls. These attacks were usually accompanied by, as Barbaro wrote, "shouting which truly was heard as far as the coast of Anatolia, twelve miles [19 km] from the Turkish camp . . . and with the sound of their castanets and tambourines, it was a thing not to be believed."

Barbaro was impressed with the bravery of the Turkish soldiers. "[As we] shot at them with guns and crossbows . . . there came other Turks and took them away, none fearing death, but being willing to let ten of themselves be killed rather than suffer the shame of leaving a single Turkish corpse by the walls."

During the siege, Ottoman ships attacked the walls of Constantinople and prevented supplies from reaching the city.

Not having succeeded in tearing down the walls, the Turks tried to mine under them. The Turkish general Zaganos Pasha had brought in experts from Serbia's silver mines for this work. They directed tunneling projects in several places. Byzantine noble Lucas Notaras and an engineer named Johannes Grant were in charge of thwarting the Turks in the tunnels. They dug countermines to capture or kill enemy miners. They burned out or flooded the tunnels. They tortured several prisoners to find out the mining sites and then beheaded the prisoners and tossed them over the city walls.

On May 18 or 19, the people of Constantinople were given another surprise. They awoke to see a huge wooden tower that the Turks had constructed overnight. Barbaro wrote: "This tower was made in such a way that no one would have believed that it could be done. . . . At once the Emperor came with his nobles to see this wonderful thing, and when they saw it they were like men struck dead for fear."

The tower was covered with animal hides. Inside were steps going to a platform that was at least as high as the top of the wall. There were scaling ladders inside, and soldiers protected by the tower were filling in the moat. The soldiers built a makeshift road across part of the moat and wheeled the tower onto it.

Nothing could be done to prevent the Ottomans' relentless progress throughout the long and tense day. Then, as darkness fell, some of the city's defenders managed to sneak out through a small gate and light explosive powder near the tower. The tower caught fire and collapsed, killing the men inside. The Turks built several other towers. The defenders destroyed some, and the Turks withdrew the rest.

On May 23, the city's defenders saw a small ship tacking toward the Golden Horn. It slipped into the harbor that night bringing bad news. This was the same ship that had set out twenty days earlier in search of help. The Venetian captain reported that he had searched the islands in the Aegean Sea, and no other ships were harbored there waiting to come to Constantinople. His crew volunteered to return to the city.

The city they returned to was filled with disunity. The Venetians and the Greeks argued over the best way to defend the city. Both groups mistrusted the Genoese, since the Genoese colony at Galata/Pera had—at best—remained neutral. Some thought, like Barbaro, that the Genoese may have secretly helped Mehmed II and his soldiers. Supplies were dangerously low. Soldiers had begun to abandon their posts. Riots and demonstrations threatened the city.

"ALL VERY BRAVE MEN"

By the end of May 1453, the defenders worried that prophesies predicting the fall of Constantinople were coming true. One stated that the city's last emperor, like its first, would be named Constantine, son of Helena—and the mother of Constantine XI was indeed Empress Helena. Another noted that the city would not fall until the full moon gave a sign. And on the night of the full moon, according to Barbaro, the moon "rose as if it were no more than a three-day moon, with only a little of it showing . . . and gradually increased to a full circle"—an eclipse. A large icon of the Virgin Mary slipped from its platform, a sudden thunderstorm with hail caused flooding in the city, and a strange light appeared over the dome of Hagia Sophia. All were taken as messages of doom.

The siege had also taken its toll on the Turks. Despite their overwhelming numbers, impressive cannons, and other

"But the thing I wonder at . . . is this: the parallelism of names occurring in the changed circumstances, while the City went on for . . . nearly 1200 years. For Constantine, the fortunate Emperor, son of Helen, built her and brought her to the pitch of happiness and fortune. And now again, under Constantine, the unfortunate emperor, son of Helen, she is taken and reduced to the worst slavery and misfortune."

—Kritovoulos (fifteenth-century Greek chronicler)

war machines, Mehmed II's army had not yet entered the city. A defeat would be humiliating. Rumor was that a fleet of rescue ships was coming from Venice, although this was not true. Some of the sultan's ministers—particularly his father's well-respected vizier, Halil Pasha—wanted to end the siege.

Mehmed II informed Constantine XI that the Turks would lift the siege if the emperor paid an annual tribute in gold or if the people still inside the city walls took only their movable possessions and abandoned it, without destroying the buildings. Constantine XI and his council of advisers decided that neither option was acceptable. He refused to leave.

The sultan consulted his ministers again. Halil Pasha again demanded that the siege be lifted. Mehmed II told his general Zaganos Pasha to ask the soldiers. Zaganos returned to say that the entire army favored an immediate attack, and the sultan agreed. Someone in the Turkish camp—perhaps Halil—wrapped a message around an arrow and shot it over the city walls. The message warned of the sultan's plans.

Mehmed II then rode through the camp to order a final assault. His aide announced that the soldiers would be allowed the customary three days to sack the city for treasure. Any soldier or sailor unable to do so because of his duties would receive his fair share.

On Sunday night, May 27, the Turks worked feverishly to fill the moat by the city walls with dirt and debris. As they readied their weapons, they sang and played battle music. At midnight all was silent. Monday would be a day of contemplation and rest.

On the last day before battle, Mehmed II inspected his troops, met with advisers, and cautioned officials in

This fresco, painted in 1537 on the walls of a Romanian monastery, shows the procession of Christians carrying icons around the city walls of Constantinople.

Galata/Pera to remain neutral. In Constantinople the church bells rang and a long procession carried icons around the city walls. Christians of all persuasions thronged into Hagia Sophia and celebrated Mass together. For the moment, it seemed, the centuries-long schism between the Greek and Latin churches had been healed.

After the church service, the emperor and his ministers asked forgiveness from one another. Giustiniani and all the remaining soldiers took their final positions between the inner wall at the Lycus Valley—where the Turks were sure to attack—and the outer stockade. Gates on the inner wall were closed behind them. There could be no retreat.

Heavy rains fell that night. At about midnight, Constantine XI took a final tour of the walls with George Sphrantzes and then dismissed him from his duties.

MAY 29, 1453

At about one thirty on Tuesday morning, May 29, the assault began. Battle cries, drums, castanets, and trumpets resounded throughout the valley. Church bells pealed a warning. All who were able went to the walls to help with repairs. Others went to church to pray.

Mehmed II's battle plan was simple and effective—tire the defenders, using the most expendable men, and save the best troops for last. First to attack the walls were the bashi-bazouks, thousands of the self-armed, poorly trained men, many from the Balkans. They carried scaling ladders and attacked in several areas along the wall to keep the defenders away from the main battle in the Lycus Valley section.

Military police behind the bashi-bazouks urged the men forward and beat those who tried to retreat. After two hours of fighting, the few bashi-bazouks left alive were ordered to withdraw. They had done their part to tire the defenders.

Next, the regular army, well armed, disciplined, and mostly from Anatolia, advanced into the Lycus Valley. Urban's monster cannon and other guns pounded the walls there. The defenders barely had time to make a few repairs before the Ottoman army started to scale the walls.

After another two hours, the janissaries marched onto the field in double time and in perfectly ordered ranks. Mehmed II led them as far as the moat. Barbaro remembers their bright

This miniature painting depicts the Ottoman forces crossing the moat and attempting to scale the walls of Constantinople on May 29, 1453.

white turbans and describes them as "all very brave men . . . [who] attacked . . . like lions, with such shouting and sounding of castanets that it seemed a thing not of this world."

The exhausted defenders had fought for more than four hours straight. They defended the city against the janissaries for another hour. It seemed as if this final attack would not succeed and that victory would go to Constantinople's defenders after all.

Then someone noticed a small gate—the Kerkoporta— at the northwest corner of the city. This rarely used gate had been opened recently to allow defenders to slip out among the enemy. Most likely a returning defender had forgotten to close it. The Turks saw the Kerkoporta was ajar. They rushed through. The defenders managed to push most of them back, but about fifty enemy soldiers had made their way inside. An unguarded gate, which had been the means for the Byzantines to recapture their city from Latin rulers nearly two hundred years earlier, would lead to the Byzantines' defeat.

As the sun rose, someone shot the city's military leader, Giovanni Giustiniani, at close range, piercing his armor. Gravely wounded, he insisted on leaving the battlefield and being taken to his ship. As a gate was opened for Longo to get into the city, panic ensued and some of the defenders abandoned their posts.

Mehmed II ordered his janissaries to renew their attack. The defenders were finally overwhelmed. One of the conquerors climbed the tower above the Kerkoporta, cut down the city's flags, and raised the Ottoman banner.

Constantinople had fallen at last.

SPOILS OF WAR

Signals flashed throughout the Turkish camp that the great walls of Constantinople had been breached. Ottoman soldiers rushed toward the city. Sailors on the Turkish warships in the Golden Horn attacked the harbor wall and met little resistance. Fishing families opened the gates to their section of city when the attackers promised that their homes would be spared.

Refugees crowded onto ships. Among them was Nicolo Barbaro. A stiff north wind helped them sail to freedom.

Giustiniani had made it on board his vessel, but he died a day or two later.

Sailors on the two ships from Crete continued to fight from towers they held near the harbor entrance. When these sailors finally surrendered, enemy officers were so impressed with their bravery that they allowed the men to return home safely.

No one knows what happened to Byzantine emperor Constantine XI. Some say he galloped into the Lycus Valley and tried to rally the defenders. Others say that he stripped off his royal insignia and charged into the oncoming Turks. Mehmed II later decided that a corpse wearing a sock with an eagle embroidered on it was the body of the emperor. The fate of that corpse is shrouded in legend, but it is unlikely that Mehmed II released it to the Greeks for burial.

The sultan returned to his tent and met with people from Constantinople and Galata/Pera who were seeking to safeguard family and property. Local officials of districts that surrendered at once were escorted to his tent with the keys to their section of the city. The sultan protected their districts and the city's second-largest cathedral from pillage. Much of the city, including Hagia Sophia, received no such protection.

Soon after the wall was breached, each Ottoman regiment marched into Constantinople with music playing and military banners flying. Once inside the city, the soldiers were free to do as they wished, except in those districts that had quickly surrendered. They rushed to Hagia Sophia, battered down the doors, killed or captured the worshippers inside, and carried off whatever valuables they could find.

A Romanian fresco shows the killing of worshippers at Hagia Sophia in 1453.

Soon little flags marked buildings that had been plundered. From his ship, Barbaro wrote: "As far as I can estimate, there would have been two hundred thousand of these flags flying in the houses all over Constantinople . . . and all through the day the Turks made a great slaughter of Christians through the city. The blood flowed in the city like rainwater in the gutters after a sudden storm, and the corpses of Turks and Christians were thrown into the Dardanelles, where they floated out to sea like melons along a canal." An estimated thirty thousand to fifty thousand people were captured. Another four thousand or so were killed.

According to an Ottoman official named Tursun Beg, the troops also "took silver and gold vessels, precious stones, and all sorts of valuable goods and fabrics from the imperial palace and the houses of the rich. In this fashion many people were delivered from poverty and made rich. Every tent was filled with handsome boys and beautiful girls."

In the late afternoon, Mehmed II mounted a white horse and rode with his ministers into the city he had longed to conquer. Although it was customary for a victorious army to have three days to pillage conquered territory, most of the looting and slaughter was already over. The janissaries who escorted the sultan established military order. Mehmed Fatih dismounted in front of Hagia Sophia. He bent down and poured a handful of dirt over his turban as a sign of humility. Inside the church, a Turkish soldier was chipping away at a mosaic. The sultan ordered him to stop. The people and treasures of Constantinople could belong to their conquerors, but the buildings would belong to Mehmed II. The few priests left in Hagia Sophia were sent away under the sultan's protection. An Ottoman religious leader proclaimed the place holy to Allah. Hagia Sophia became the Aya Sofya mosque.

CHAPTER SIX

ISTANBUL AND EMPIRE

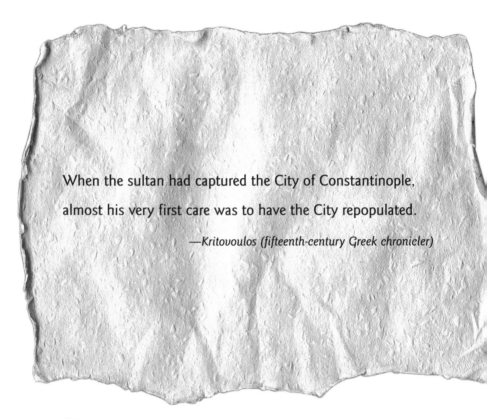

When the sultan had captured the City of Constantinople, almost his very first care was to have the City repopulated.

—*Kritovoulos (fifteenth-century Greek chronicler)*

By the end of the pillaging on May 29, 1453, there was little left of value that had not already been claimed by the Ottoman troops. That evening Mehmed II ordered the looting to cease. The next day, he redistributed booty to those who couldn't participate in the sack of the city and he took a share for himself. The sultan freed most of the women of high-ranking, wealthy families so that they could find enough money and jewels to redeem family members, but he kept many of their children.

George Sphrantzes and his family were captured. After eighteen months as a slave to one of the sultan's officials, Sphrantzes paid for his freedom and was able to redeem his wife, but he was unable to redeem his two children. Sphrantzes wrote that in December 1453, "the most impious and pitiless sultan, with his own hand, took the life of my dearest son John, on the grounds that the child had conspired to murder him. Alas for me, his unfortunate and wretched father! My son was fourteen years and eight months less a day; yet his mind and body proclaimed a much more mature person." The next year, his fourteen-year-old daughter Thamar "died of an infectious disease in the sultan's seraglio [area for women]."

Mehmed II executed other officials, including the nobleman named Lucas Notaras. Notaras's daughter Anna escaped to Italy with the family's treasures and started a new life there. Cardinal Isidore traded clothes with a beggar who was mistaken for the cardinal and decapitated. Isidore was later captured and sold as a slave. A merchant from Galata/Pera recognized the cardinal, bought him, and then helped him escape to Italy as well.

Since Galata/Pera had opened its gates to his soldiers, the sultan granted it the status of a Christian town submitting to voluntary rule. No pillaging or slave taking was allowed. The people of Galata/Pera, including the Genoese, paid taxes to their newly installed Turkish governor, did not ring church bells, and refrained from building any new churches.

In June Mehmed II returned briefly to his castle at Adrianople. Representatives from Serbia and nearby Venetian colonies came with gifts and requests for peaceful alliances. They included an envoy from the Knights of Saint John, a Catholic religious order on Rhodes, an island off the southwest coast of Anatolia. He explained that the knights could not pay anything or acknowledge his authority without the pope's permission. The sultan decided to leave these knights alone for the moment.

With the siege over, Mehmed II consolidated his power. He executed Halil Pasha and made Zaganos Pasha grand vizier. The janissaries continued to back Mehmed. His goals now were to rebuild Constantinople as the capital of the Ottoman Empire and to expand that empire all the way to Rome.

Constantinople was not only a key link between Europe and Asia, but it also was the seat of Orthodox Christianity. Its loss to Christendom was interpreted in several ways. The Venetian surgeon Nicolo Barbaro wrote: "[O]ur Lord decided . . . that He was willing for the city to fall . . . in order to fulfill all the ancient prophesies." The patriarch of the Orthodox Church in Russia declared that Constantinople had been punished for contemplating unity with the Catholics. It proved that Russian Orthodoxy was the true faith.

Constantinople's former patriarch, Gregory Mammas, had sought to unite with the Church of Rome, and he had left Constantinople in 1451. The Orthodox clergy in Constantinople had not elected anyone to replace him during the two years before Constantinople fell to the Turks. Mehmed II could have let that position remain vacant. Instead, he sought out the well-respected Greek Orthodox monk George Gennadius Scholarius. Mehmed found Gennadius near Adrianople among the slaves of a prosperous Turk who had treated him well.

Gennadius became the new patriarch in January 1454 in a ceremony used in Constantinople for centuries. But this time, it was a Muslim sultan rather than Christian emperor who gave Gennadius his official robes and cross—which Mehmed II provided since the old cross had disappeared.

A few months later, Gennadius moved from the Holy Apostles Cathedral, in a Turkish community, to the smaller church in Phanar, a Greek section of the city. There the sultan created a Greek Orthodox *millet*—a self-governing community within the Ottoman Empire. Gennadius and his bishops controlled church-related matters, such as marriage and the guardianship of children, based on Justinian's codification of Roman law. The patriarch was responsible to the sultan, however, and Turkish courts handled all criminal cases and any case involving a Muslim. Turkish officials collected taxes, and janissaries policed the city.

By supporting the Greek Orthodox Church, the Muslims strengthened a religious community that had been under pressure from the Church of Rome. Constantinople's Christian Orthodox religious leaders gained authority and some autonomy throughout much of the Ottoman Empire, including areas of the Balkans where the predominant religious sect was Serbian Orthodox.

EUROPE'S RESPONSE

Europe was slow to learn of the Ottoman victory and even slower to respond. Messengers finally got to Venice a month after the siege ended, and a courier reached the pope in Rome on July 8. Meanwhile, the Venetian ships that the pope had sent to defend Constantinople had reached Chios, an island in the Aegean Sea. Genoese ships from Galata/Pera met them there and told them it was too late. The Venetian admiral moved his fleet into Venetian-controlled waters.

Venetian leaders heard testimony from Alvise Diedo, the captain of the ships defending Constantinople, and they were shocked by the news. Soon afterward, the senate in Venice sent an ambassador, Bartolomeo Marcello, to Mehmed II. Marcello's job was to get the sultan to release those Venetian merchant ships remaining in Constantinople. The Greeks still owed Venice money for the supplies purchased for the defense of the city. Venice wanted any merchandise confiscated from these ships in payment for its losses.

Marcello was also supposed to negotiate a treaty with the Ottomans to ensure peaceful trade. Meanwhile, others in Venice were trying to organize a crusade to recapture Constantinople. Marcello eventually arranged a truce, redeemed some captives and merchant ships, and gained trading privileges. But in 1456, he was called back to Venice where, to show that Venice was the enemy of the infidel Ottomans, he was thrown into prison.

In September 1453, Pope Nicholas V issued a papal bull urging all the nobles of Europe to join in a crusade against the Ottoman Turks. But Germany's Emperor Frederick III didn't have the money or troops. His cousin, King Ladislas of Hungary, had problems with his military leaders. England and France were recovering from their Hundred Years War (1337–1453) against each other, and King Alfonso of

Aragon (in Spain) had trouble enough keeping land he controlled in Italy.

Philip the Good, the duke of Burgundy and possibly the richest nobleman in Europe, held a banquet in February 1454, where he promised to pay for a crusade. But the duke did little, Pope Nicholas V died a year later, and an army never materialized.

For two centuries, Roman Catholic popes had blamed Greek Orthodox patriarchs for dividing the Christian Church. It was difficult to get Catholic Europe to undertake another crusade on their behalf. In 1459 a later pope named the Catholic cardinal Isidore as the patriarch of Constantinople in defiance of Orthodox traditions. The pope thought this would be a way to unify the churches—despite the fact that the Orthodox bishops had already elected their own patriarch for Constantinople.

Ottoman diplomats soon learned that Europe would not unite against them. Mehmed II could wage war on his neighbors one at a time, with little worry about a crusade. And so he did.

REBUILDING ON A GRAND SCALE

In the decade after the fall of Constantinople, the Ottoman Turks wiped out almost all that remained of the Byzantine Empire. They occupied lands Constantine XI had given to his two brothers (Demetrius and Thomas) when he became emperor of Byzantium, other colonies in the Aegean Sea, and the duchy of Athens. Only in a few places, such as the island of Cyprus, were Greeks still ruled by Greeks.

Marching eastward into Anatolia, Mehmed II's men attacked Trebizond, ruled by Byzantine emperor David. The emperor joined forces with Uzun Hasan, a Muslim leader of a tribe of Turks who opposed the Ottomans. Mehmed II forced Uzan Hasan into a truce, and David finally surrendered. Trebizond fell on August 15, 1461. The Ottoman army also conquered the rival Turkish state of Karaman.

The young sultan, in his twenties, was determined that Constantine's once-great city would become the capital of a vast and prosperous Ottoman Empire. He called his new capital Istanbul, based on a Turkish reference to the city, and set about restoring it on a grand scale. But Istanbul did not have enough people to run the new government, establish a thriving trade in European and Asian goods, and raise crops to feed the empire. As the empire spread, more

Emperor David of Trebizond surrendered to Mehmed II in 1461, giving the Ottomans control of all of Anatolia. A fifteenth-century Italian artist painted this scene of the conquest of Trebizond.

THE CITY

For hundreds of years, Greeks officially referred to the capital of their empire as Konstantinoupolis (the city of Constantine) or Nea Roma (New Rome). Bulgarians, Russians, and Serbs referred to this same place as Tsarigrad—"the city of emperors." But many Greeks simply called it *polis*, meaning "city." To them there was only one important city, just as some people refer to New York City as the City. The Turkish peasants of Anatolia commonly thought of Constantinople in the same way. Their name was a corruption of the Greek phrase meaning "into the city"—*eis ten polin*, or Istanbul. The city officially was renamed Istanbul in 1930.

Ottomans were needed to govern in other regions and to ensure that newly conquered territories did not rebel.

The sultan's solution was the forced transfer and resettlement of populations within his empire. Ashikpashazade, a historian who lived at that time, wrote that Mehmed II "sent his servants to all his lands, to say: 'Whoever wishes, let him come, and let him become owner of houses, vineyards and gardens in Istanbul.' And they gave them to all who came. This, however, was not enough to repopulate the city." The sultan's officers then "conscripted and brought very many families" against their will.

Mehmed II also ordered his government ministers to build their homes in his new capital. He had inns, baths,

"[The sultan raised] an immense storm upon the Christians and upon his own people by transporting them from place to place. . . . I composed this in times of bitterness, for they brought us from Amasya to Konstandnupolis [sic] by force and against our will; and I copied this tearfully with much lamentation."

—Nerses (Armenian merchant), 1480

marketplaces, mosques, and other public buildings erected, as well. Artisans, jewelers, metalworkers, merchants, and many other tradespeople had also been forced to move to the capital. He restored the great market areas, built Yedi Kule (Seven Towers), a huge fortress that held treasure and valuable captives, and started Topkapi Palace, a large walled compound in the southeast part of the city. Topkapi Palace would be the home of the Ottoman sultans for nearly four hundred years.

Mehmed II continued the Ottoman practice of gathering boys from among the conquered peoples and raising them in the service of the sultan. Many of these boys later held prestigious and prosperous positions in government or joined the janissaries. Islam's religious laws forbade the enslavement of Muslims, but the sultan's ministers interpreted that as Muslims of Turkish origin only. Muslim Slavs could be gathered.

The Ottoman army marched north and west into Europe too. They captured most of Serbia. They attempted a siege of Belgrade in 1456 but were unsuccessful. Later the Ottomans captured Bosnia and Albania. The Ottoman

SLAVES OF THE GATE

Traditionally the sultan's officials carried out the governing of the empire from the front portion or gate of the sultan's palace. Many of these officials, as well as the sultan's soldiers, had been gathered and enslaved from non-Muslim peoples. The officials were called *kapi kulu*, or "slaves of the gate." Slaves of the gate were often held in high esteem and treated well. After the conquest of Bosnia in 1463, conquered Muslim Slavs received permission to become slaves of the gate even though the Quran forbids enslavement of Muslims.

Empire vied with Venice for control of trade routes and military might. Venice took back some Ottoman lands in 1463, but Mehmed II improved his navy, recaptured lost territory in 1467, and continued to wage war on the Venetians.

During the summer of 1467, according to Sphrantzes, "the plague overwhelmed Constantinople [and elsewhere]. . . . They say that tens of thousands, not merely thousands, of human beings perished." The outbreak of the plague hit other cities and towns in the region as well.

Mehmed II forged military and political alliances whenever that fit with his ultimate goal of expanding the Ottoman Empire. The sultan sent his troops to the Tatars—the Mongol group that had fought with the Ottomans fifty years earlier—to help them defend against attacks by Poland, Moldavia, and Muscovy (part of Russia). The Tatars helped the Ottomans keep the northern ports of the Black Sea out of enemy hands.

The forces of Mehmed II attempted a siege of Belgrade (in modern Serbia) in 1456 but failed to conquer the city. This image is of a miniature painting from the Topkapi Museum in Istanbul.

Beginning in 1475, the Tatars accepted Ottoman rule for nearly three hundred years and became some of the best soldiers in the Ottoman army.

Expanding an empire and rebuilding the imperial city cost money. Mehmed II imposed heavy taxes, raised customs duties on goods shipped through Ottoman territory, and seized land. He forcibly exchanged old coins for new ones at five-sixths their value to get more valuable coins in his treasury.

Not everyone in the Turkish Muslim community agreed with his actions. Old rivalries smoldered between the Ottomans and other groups. The sultan relied more and more heavily on the "gathered" Christians (who were converted to Islam) in his administration. Most of his political leaders, including grand viziers, were these former Christians.

Mehmed II brought scientists and artists from Europe and Asia to his capital city. A great astronomer of that time—a Persian named Ali Kuscu of Samarkand—taught at the school Mehmed II established beside Aya Sofya. The sultan studied Christianity with the help of patriarch Gennadius, attended scholarly lectures, and read books on Greek philosophy.

In 1477 Mehmed II ordered a census of Constantinople and Galata/Pera. Results showed about eighty thousand inhabitants, excluding "slaves of the Gate"—an amazing increase from the seven thousand or so able-bodied defenders (not including Galata/Pera) counted in 1453. Census takers listed 9,486 houses inhabited by Muslims, 3,743 houses inhabited by Greeks, 1,647 houses inhabited by Jews, 434 houses inhabited by Armenians, 384 houses inhabited by Karamanians (a Turkish tribe), 332 houses inhabited by Franks (western Europeans including Italians), 267 houses inhabited by

This engraving of a view of Constantinople at the end of the fifteenth century is from the Nuremberg Chronicle, *a book written in Latin and German versions by Hartmann Schedel in 1493.*

Christians from the Crimea (a peninsula on the northern coast of the Black Sea), and 31 houses inhabited by Gypsies.

Official political divisions within the city were set up according to religions. Within these millets, communities often had their own distinct customs, language, and style of architecture. "Greeks" referred to those whose allegiances were to the Greek Orthodox Church and included many Serbians. Muslims might come from Black Sea towns or Syrian cities. Jews might be from Germany, Genoa, and elsewhere. Istanbul had become a truly international city.

According to Islamic law, Christians and Jews who paid their taxes were considered *zimmi* (protected persons) because of a shared heritage with Islam. They had the right to worship and to live by their own civil and religious laws. The Jewish community had fewer restrictions in Istanbul

MEHMED'S JEWISH DOCTOR

The sultan's personal physician and trusted adviser was a man named Yakub Pasha. He was also known as Giacomo di Gaeta, or Jacob of Gaeta—an Italian Jew who sought a better life in the Ottoman Empire and who is said to have converted to Islam. Yakub Pasha had such a high position in the sultan's court that he sometimes was used as a spy to convey disinformation to the sultan's enemies. Mehmed II granted Yakub a tax exemption for himself and his descendants, regardless of whether they were Muslim or Jewish.

and elsewhere in the Ottoman Empire than they had in most parts of western Europe.

NEXT STOP, ROME?

In 1479, after Ottoman troops had conquered nearly all its territory, Venice surrendered. The peace treaty required Venice to pay an annual tribute to the sultan and allowed Venetians to trade within the Ottoman Empire. Soon afterward, the famous Venetian artist Gentile Bellini visited the sultan and painted his portrait.

The conquest of Constantinople established the Ottomans as one of the great powers of Europe. Mehmed II ruled an empire from the Danube River in the Balkans well into Anatolia in the east. But Mehmed the

The Venetian artist Gentile Bellini visited Mehmed II in the late fifteenth century and painted this portrait of him.

Conqueror was said to still have his heart set on another ancient city—Rome.

In 1480 Ottoman troops captured Otranto in southern Italy and started northward toward Rome. The pope prepared to retreat to France. Mehmed II, meanwhile, was leading other military forces eastward from Istanbul into Asia.

Although only forty-nine, the sultan was reported to look unusually thin and weak. While leading his troops, he died on May 3, 1481, possibly from poison. His death brought an end to the Ottoman march on Rome.

Mehmed II's armies returned to Istanbul, where rivalries between the janissaries and Turkish high officials raged. The janissaries threw their support behind Mehmed II's older son, Bayezid II, and succeeded in making him sultan. Mehmed II's younger son, Cem, sought protection from the Knights of Saint John on the island of Rhodes. Bayezid II later paid for Cem to be kept in France and Italy—and to be treated well—until Cem's death in 1495.

The Ottoman Empire under Bayezid II expanded only a little, but it prospered. Trade grew, the tax system improved, and Ottoman power in the Black Sea region increased.

In 1512 Bayezid II's son, Selim, overthrew his father and killed his brothers. Selim expanded the empire eastward by attacking the Safavids, a Persian dynasty that was founded by a Muslim mystic in the thirteenth century. He also conquered the Mamluks, a rival Muslim group originally from the Black Sea region, and took control of the Islamic holy cities of Medina and Mecca in Arabia.

Most importantly, Selim brought Syria (which then included Israel, Palestine, and Lebanon) and Egypt into the

TULIPS

The Ottomans enjoyed the brilliant colors of hardy six-pointed flowers native to Anatolia, flowers known in English as tulips. Mehmed II and later sultans cultivated huge tulip gardens. An ambassador from the Austrian king brought tulip bulbs back to Europe in the sixteenth century. By the seventeenth century, tulips were so popular in the Netherlands that a single bulb might cost as much as a house.

empire. All major trade routes between Asia and Europe then fell within Ottoman territory. The Ottomans controlled the coffee trade from Egypt and the great caravans that traveled through the deserts of the Middle East. They also had commercial ties with merchants from Europe, who paid for the privilege of living in Istanbul or trading with merchants there. The empire prospered through the taxes traders paid to ship their goods.

Before his death in 1520, Selim killed all of his sons except one—Suleyman I, whose rule would last for forty-six years. Selim left Suleyman a large and powerful empire and no immediate threat to the throne.

SULEYMAN'S MAGNIFICENT EMPIRE

The new sultan became known in Europe as Suleyman the Magnificent, in part because of the splendor of his court and of Istanbul. The city had grown from the crumbling ruins that Mehmed II conquered in 1453 to a thriving metropolis. Tradespeople and merchants gathered daily at the Grand Bazaar, a forerunner of modern shopping malls. There were public gardens, elaborate public baths, and grand mosques.

One of the five main pillars, or religious duties, of Islam is charity. Wealthier families could reduce or eliminate their taxes by giving money to a *vakif* (charitable foundation). Many poorer people benefited from this practice. The sultan was also expected to show his greatness in part by providing for the poor. The huge mosque Suleyman built was a complex of structures that included a library, an orphanage, a kitchen for the poor, and a caravansary (a kind of hostel for caravans of camels and their riders).

Istanbul had schools and colleges dedicated to educating boys and young men. Young boys and sometimes girls were usually tutored at home. Then the boys attended a *medrese* (school attached to a mosque) and also learned a trade. Most girls continued to be

An Italian painter made this portrait of Suleyman in 1550. He was known as Suleyman the Magnificent because of the beauty of his attire and the splendor of his court.

A group of boys attending a medrese in the early nineteenth century was painted by French artist Alexandre-Gabriel Decamps.

taught basic and household skills and were married off at the age of twelve or so.

By Ottoman law, each major religious community wore distinctive clothing. Only Muslims were allowed to wear white or green turbans and yellow slippers. Jews and Christians were required to wear dark colors or blue. Most men wore simple robes with a padded outer garment in colder weather. Women usually covered themselves with long coats and veils whenever they went outside. The coat of a wealthier woman might be fur trimmed. The women wore soft-soled shoes on wooden stilts when walking though muddy street. Inside the houses and public baths, women wore dresses and wide pants.

The arts flourished under Suleyman's rule. The sultan wrote poetry and encouraged others to do so. He gave

The huge Suleymaniye Mosque, built by Suleyman, was a complex of buildings for worshipping, learning, and providing for travelers and the poor. The mosque still stands in Istanbul.

particular support to calligraphy (decorative handwriting), painting in miniature, textile crafts, and tile making. Craftspeople in Istanbul joined guilds to teach others their skills and regulate the prices of their goods.

During Suleyman's time, the administrators of the Ottoman Empire governed from the many offices in the Topkapi Palace. There was one minister of finance for Rumeli (Roman) lands—the European half of the empire, including the Balkans—and another for Anatolia and parts of Asia. Christians, Jews, and other non-Muslims paid a special tax. They were not allowed to own slaves, live near mosques, or build tall buildings.

The janissaries and other "gathered" men dominated all political and military functions during Suleyman's rule. So many of the gathered were from the Balkans that a French traveler in the 1540s remarked that Serbo-Croatian was spoken more often among the palace guards than Turkish. Though formerly Christian, the Slavic janissaries often disagreed with the policies of the Greek-dominated Orthodox patriarchs and their bishops.

The Turks called Suleyman Kanuni, meaning the "lawgiver." Like Justinian I, one thousand years earlier, one of the sultan's greatest achievements was the codification of laws. Many of these laws dealt with taxation and use of land. The laws also included issues that were decided by religious judges.

The empire expanded under Suleyman as well. In the West, the Ottoman Empire bordered on the territory

The Topkapi Palace in Istanbul was the administrative center of Suleyman's empire. This view is from a fresco in the palace museum.

controlled by the Hapsburgs. The Hapsburg family originally ruled Austria and gradually gained dominance over other parts of Europe. It called itself the Holy Roman Empire. Hungary was the battleground between the Ottoman and the Hapsburg empires. Suleyman invaded Hungary and tried unsuccessfully to capture Vienna, the Austrian capital. Austria remained in Hapsburg hands, but Suleyman gained control of Hungary.

SOKOLOVIC—SOKOLLU

Sokollu Mehmed Pasha was taken from his native town of Visegrad in Bosnia as part of the devshirme system. Through this practice, the Ottomans collected young boys from conquered lands who then served as janissaries or in the Ottoman government. Born Bajica Sokolovic in 1505, Sokollu Mehmed Pasha rose through the ranks of the imperial goverment to become grand vizier of the Ottoman Empire from 1564 to 1579. He was a brilliant statesman, and he made many important political and military decisions for the sultans. It is said that he ran the government under the reign of Selim II, who was not as capable as his father, Suleyman.

Sokollu Mehmed Pasha kept up his ties to his Slavic family and had them appointed to government positions. He also reinstituted the religious post of archbishop for Serbia (then including Bosnia). The patriarch in Constantinople objected, but Sokollu Mehmed Pasha prevailed. The first archbishop for Serbia was Sokollu's brother.

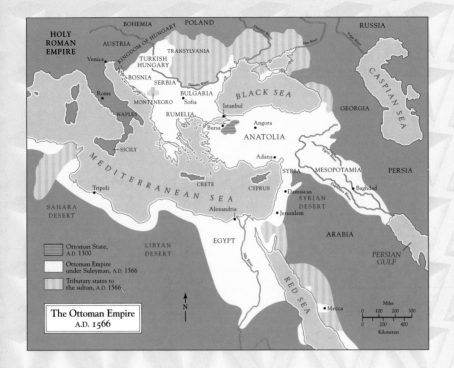

HOLY ROMAN EMPIRE

Venice

Rome

NAPLES

SICILY

AUSTRIA

BOHEMIA

KINGDOM OF HUNGARY

TURKISH HUNGARY

BOSNIA

SERBIA

MONTENEGRO

RUMELIA

POLAND

TRANSYLVANIA

Danube River

BULGARIA

Sofia

Istanbul

Bursa

Dnistr River

BLACK SEA

ANATOLIA

Angora

RUSSIA

Don River

Volga River

CASPIAN SEA

GEORGIA

MEDITERRANEAN SEA

Tripoli

CRETE

CYPRUS

Adana

SYRIA

Damascus

SYRIAN DESERT

Jerusalem

MESOPOTAMIA

Tigris River

Euphrates River

Baghdad

PERSIA

SAHARA DESERT

Alexandria

ARABIA

PERSIAN GULF

LIBYAN DESERT

EGYPT

Nile River

White Nile

Blue Nile

RED SEA

Mecca

Ottoman State, A.D. 1300

Ottoman Empire under Suleyman, A.D. 1566

Tributary states to the sultan, A.D. 1566

The Ottoman Empire
A.D. 1566

N

Miles
0   100   200   300
0   200   400
Kilometers

After the conflict in the West was temporarily settled,
the Ottomans once again turned against the Safavids in the
East. Suleyman captured Baghdad and Basra, in present-day
Iraq. By the time of the sultan's death in 1566, the
Ottomans controlled almost all the Middle East. And at the
center of their empire was the ancient city of Byzantium-
Constantinople-Istanbul.

CHAPTER SEVEN

CITY OF THE WORLD'S DESIRE

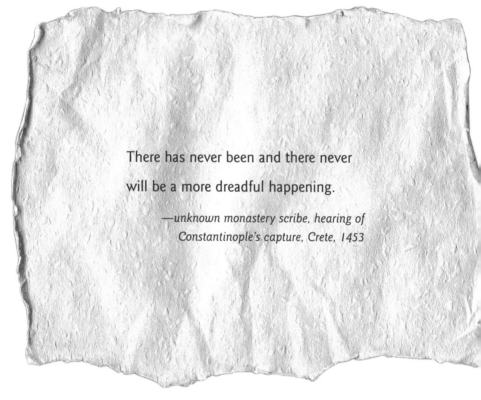

There has never been and there never
will be a more dreadful happening.

—*unknown monastery scribe, hearing of*
Constantinople's capture, Crete, 1453

The Ottoman sultans who followed Suleyman did not match
his greatness. Suleyman's Russian wife Hurrem (or Roxelana)
had had great influence over her husband. She arranged for the
deaths of Suleyman's sons by other wives, leaving only her own.
The least able of all of them, Selim, inherited the throne. This
would often be the case throughout the rest of the Ottoman
rule. Intrigue among the sultan's wives and administrators,
rather than ability to govern, determined who would become

sultan. Despite poor governance, the Ottoman Empire lasted another 350 years. The lands once ruled by the Byzantine emperors—including present-day Greece—were often the battlegrounds between the Ottomans and the other major power in the region, Venice. Some Greeks continue to keep alive the hope of once again ruling their homeland. In 1812 they formed a society to stir uprisings against the Ottomans.

The Greeks staged a revolution that lasted from 1821 to 1832, when Britain, France, and Russia—known as the Powers—united with them against the Turks to carve out a small independent Greek kingdom. Istanbul remained under

Between 1821 and 1832, the Greek people rebelled against their Turkish overlords. This Greek painting from the period depicts an early battle at Alamana Bridge.

the control of the Ottoman Turks. The country of Greece was created as a protectorate of the Powers. It was ruled by Otho I, the teenage son of the king of Bavaria.

YOUNG TURKS AND A NEW TURKEY

At the end of the nineteenth century, a group called the Committee of Union and Progress—later known as the Young Turks—tried to make the empire more democratic. By 1909 they had succeeded. The sultan was still the head of state, but the empire was governed by an elected parliament, or legislature—a constitutional monarchy. Over the next few years, Italy, Bulgaria, Serbia, Greece, and Montenegro captured parts of Ottoman territory.

By the start of World War I (1914–1918), the Ottoman Empire was basically reduced to the region around Istanbul, parts of eastern Thrace and western Anatolia, including Armenia. During the war, the Turks forcibly removed Armenians (at least in the hundreds of thousands) from their homes and many died.

Mehmed Vahideddin VI was the last Ottoman sultan. He died in exile in Rome in 1926.

The sultan reluctantly sided with Germany and Austria-Hungary in World War I. He was defeated by the Allied powers—including France, Great Britain, and the United States. Greece had entered the war on the side of the Allies. The victorious Allies arranged to give much of the remaining Ottoman territory to Greece in a peace agreement signed by the Ottoman government in Sèvres, France, in 1920. But the treaty never came into effect.

A former Ottoman army officer, Mustafa Kemal, led a group that fought to establish a new government to represent the people of Turkey. They attacked the Greek army

ARE TURKEYS FROM TURKEY?

The English thought so. In about Shakespeare's time (1500s), merchants from the eastern Mediterranean area, then part of the Ottoman Empire, brought a new kind of bird to the dinner tables of England. These businessmen were called Turkey merchants, and the bird was referred to as a Turkey bird or Turkey cock. The Ottomans and many others thought that turkeys came from India, particularly an area called Calicut.

In reality, early European explorers of the Americas took turkeys from Mexico and brought them to Europe about 1520. People likely mixed up India with the New Indies, the name Columbus gave to the lands he found. The English reintroduced turkeys to the American colonies.

Mustafa Kemal (Ataturk) led Turkey as its president from 1923 until 1938. He replaced the Ottoman Turkish alphabet, written in Arabic, with a modified Latin alphabet similar to written English.

occupying Anatolia. Hostilities flared, and many thousands of Greeks and Armenians lost their lives. Under a treaty signed in 1923, Britain, France, Greece, and other nations recognized the Republic of Turkey. The treaty called for an exchange of populations. About one and a half million Orthodox Christians were expelled from Turkey and encouraged to resettle in Greece, and about half a million Muslims were transferred from Greece to Turkey. The patriarch of the Greek Orthodox Church was allowed to remain in Istanbul, and several communities of Christians and Muslims were exempt from the transfer.

Mustafa Kemal became president of Turkey, taking the name Ataturk (father Turk). The new nation shed many of its traditional Muslim and Ottoman ways. The city that Mehmed the Conqueror had desired so badly was abandoned as the capital. Ankara, held by Turkish peoples for about eight hundred years, became the new capital. Europeans had once called that

BANISHMENT

On November 1, 1922, the Grand National Assembly of the newly established Republic of Turkey abolished the sultanate. It allowed the sultan (Mehmed Vahideddin) to retain the title of caliph. Vahideddin left Istanbul for Italy, and crown prince Abdul Mecit Efendi took his place as religious leader.

On March 3, 1924, the assembly abolished the caliphate and forbade the caliph and all his descendants to live in Turkey. That night the caliph's sister, Princess Musbah, accompanied the imperial family to the train leaving for Europe.

"It was a night of bitter cold and driving rain," Musbah wrote. "[T]he entrance to the station was guarded by troops and police. It seemed to be an unnecessary precaution in view of the apathetic attitude adopted by the public toward the banishment of the House of Osman from Turkey."

city Angora—the same name as the fine, soft wool that comes from the region's goats.

The surrender of Ottoman Istanbul to Allied naval forces in World War I marked the virtual end of the six-hundred-year-old Ottoman Empire, just as Constantinople's fall to the Ottoman Turks in 1453 marked the end of the eleven-hundred-year-old Byzantine Empire. No matter what its current name might be, the city that was built on the "perfect spot" between Europe and Asia and that was the envy of Alexander the Great continues to thrive in the modern world.

LESSONS FROM AN ANCIENT CITY

The complex political history of Byzantium as well as the events surrounding the fall of Constantinople in 1453 and its immediate aftermath still reverberate in world politics. More than five centuries after the Ottomans conquered the Byzantine Empire, the Balkans continues to be a region filled

BYZANTINE BYZANTIUM

Sixteenth-century historians were likely the first to use the term *Byzantine* to apply to the empire ruled for a thousand years by Constantinople. Two centuries later, British historian Edward Gibbon (1734–1794) showed his strong bias against the Greeks of Constantinople in his popular six-volume work, *The History of the Decline and Fall of the Roman Empire*. Others shared Gibbon's views, including William Lecky (1838–1903), who wrote: "Of that Byzantine Empire the universal verdict of history is that it constitutes, without a single exception, the most thoroughly base and despicable form that civilisation has yet assumed. . . . The history of the empire is a monotonous study of the intrigues of priest, eunuchs, and women, of poisonings, of conspiracies, of uniform ingratitude, of perpetual fratricides."

Historians now recognize the achievements and importance of the Byzantine Empire. But past prejudices survive in the English adjective *Byzantine*, which is used to describe, with negative connotations, something that is complex, convoluted, knotty, intricate, or tangled.

with religious and ethnic conflicts. Some animosities developed before the Ottoman Turks controlled the Balkans. Others are between those who remained or became Christian and those who converted to Islam under Ottoman rule. Still other conflicts are based on the creation of the new political boundaries established during the breakup of the Ottoman Empire.

The treaties that ended World War I and the Ottoman Empire also created Yugoslavia, a new Slavic state that consisted of the regions of Bosnia-Herzegovina, Croatia, Macedonia, Montenegro, Serbia, and Slovenia. The Serbs quickly established dominance in Yugoslavia, antagonizing other ethnic groups, particularly the Croats, who tried to break away. Josip Broz Tito led Yugoslavia as a Communist

Josip Broz Tito controlled Yugoslavia from 1945 until his death in 1980. He is pictured here reviewing troops in 1954.

state for decades after World War II (1939–1945). Although he sometimes resorted to repression, he worked hard to maintain the multiethnic nation. After Tito's death in 1980, however, violence and bloodshed tore Yugoslavia apart.

A few years after the fall of Constantinople, Ottoman rulers of Bosnia established Sarajevo as a city, building a water-supply system, mosque, schools, and public bath. Sarajevo, capital of present-day Bosnia-Herzegovina, thrived and become known in the twentieth century for its cultural and religious diversity. As Yugoslavia disintegrated, fighting in Slavic Bosnia led to a three-year siege (1992–1995) and large-scale destruction of the ancient city. An estimated two hundred thousand people died during the fighting in Bosnia, including eight thousand Muslim men and boys killed in July 1995 in the town of Srebrenica.

Another flash point in the Balkans has been Kosovo, a region that once had a large Serbian population of Orthodox Christians until it was conquered by the Ottomans and resettled by Muslim Turks and Albanians. Fighting broke out between the Kosovo Liberation Army (KLA) and Serbian and Yugoslav security forces. This led in 1999 to war between Yugoslavia and the members of the North Atlantic Treaty Organization (NATO) and thousands of deaths. Kosovo was placed under United Nations administration.

Despite the tensions plaguing that area of the world, however, there are also signs of a more peaceful solution to conflict. Although there is still serious disagreement between Greece and Turkey—particularly over the island of Cyprus and areas of the Aegean Sea—relations between the two countries have improved. They helped each other when earthquakes hit the region in 1999 and have established a telephone hotline among their air force command centers as a way to reduce tensions over alleged violations of airspace.

Turkey has requested membership in the European Union (EU), a group of countries with political and economic ties and a single official currency, the euro. Greece, a member of the EU since 1981, once opposed Turkey's admission but has since supported Turkey's request. If Turkey is successful, it will be the first majority-Muslim country in the union.

More than 5 million immigrants of Turkish descent live in Europe, including an estimated 2.6 million in Germany (by contrast, fewer than 118,000 Turkish immigrants lived in the United States, according to the 2000 census). Many emigrated from Turkey to Germany in the past fifty years. They were officially invited into the country (then West Germany) to relieve a labor shortage. The Turks form Germany's largest Muslim community.

Christian religious leaders in Europe are also striving to reduce the schism between the Catholic and Orthodox churches, which contributed to the destruction of Constantinople in the Fourth Crusade and the fall of the city to the Ottoman Turks in 1453. The mutual excommunications that occurred in Constantinople in 1054 were finally rescinded in 1965 by Pope Paul VI and Greek Orthodox patriarch Athenagoras I.

In 2005 Pope Benedict XVI went to Bari, an ancient port city in southern Italy and once part of both the Byzantine and Ottoman empires. The pope's visit was on May 29, exactly 552 years after the fall of Constantinople. He spoke of Bari as "the land of encounter and dialogue

Pope Benedict XVI visited Bari, Italy, in 2005. It was his first papal trip outside of Vatican City after becoming pope. His visit to the town, with its close ties to Orthodox Christianity, was seen as a gesture of mending relations between Eastern Orthodoxy and Roman Catholicism.

with our Christian brothers of the East" and recalled that Bari is the burial place of a fourth-century bishop of Myra, a city in Turkey. This Christian bishop was imprisoned by the Roman emperor Diocletian and released after Constantine took the throne. One of the most popular saints in the Catholic and Greek Orthodox Churches, he is known as Saint Nicholas. In the United States, he has evolved into Santa Claus, the symbol of Christmas gift giving.

NEW BYZANTIUM

His Imperial and Royal Highness Prince Theodore IX Lascaris Comnenus, who lives in Venezuela, claims to be the current heir to the Byzantine Empire. According to his website (www.new-byzantium.org), the nations of the Western Hemisphere are the New Byzantium—where Greek civilization, Western thought, and Christian faith will continue to survive.

Although Ankara is the capital of present-day Turkey, the great city of Justinian and Suleyman—Mehmed II's "eye of the world"—remains Turkey's economic center, still straddling two continents, still with an international focus. A Byzantine writer once called Constantinople "the city of the world's desire," and today's travelers still find Istanbul a cosmopolitan city with a variety of cultures and traditions.

Cosmopolitan is a word based on two Greek words: *kosmos*, meaning "universe" or "world" and *polites*, meaning "a citizen." An Ottoman statesman once noted that a cosmopolitan place is strong because it draws "the best talents, customs and manners from among its various nations." Understanding how the fall of Constantinople happened centuries ago helps us to recognize the strength that can arise from a modern diverse society and to appreciate the potential of our cosmopolitan world.

PRIMARY SOURCE RESEARCH

To learn about historical events, people study many sources, such as books, websites, newspaper articles, photographs, and paintings. These sources can be separated into two general categories—primary sources and secondary sources.

A primary source is the record of an eyewitness. Primary sources provide firsthand accounts about a person or event. Examples include diaries, letters, autobiographies, speeches, newspapers, and oral history interviews. Libraries, archives, historical societies, and museums often have primary sources available on-site or on the Internet.

A secondary source is published information that was researched, collected, and written or otherwise created by someone who was not an eyewitness. These authors or artists use primary sources and other secondary sources in their research, but they interpret and arrange the source material in their own works. Secondary sources include history books, novels, biographies, movies, documentaries, and magazines. Libraries and museums are filled with secondary sources.

After finding primary and secondary sources, authors and historians must evaluate them. They may ask questions such as: Who created this document? What is this person's point of view? What biases might this person have? How trustworthy is this document? Just because a person was an eyewitness to an event does not mean that person recorded the whole truth about that event. For example, a soldier describing a battle might depict only the heroic actions of his unit and only the brutal behavior of the enemy. An account from a soldier on the opposing side might portray the same battle very differently. When sources disagree, researchers must decide through additional study which explanation makes the most sense. For this reason, historians consult a variety of primary and secondary sources. Then they can draw their own conclusions.

The Pivotal Moments in History series takes readers on a journey to important junctures in history that shaped our modern world. Authors researched each event using both primary and secondary sources, an approach that enhances readers' awareness of the complexities of the materials and helps bring to life the rich stories from which we draw our understanding of our shared history.

PRIMARY SOURCE DOCUMENT: AUTOBIOGRAPHY OF GEORGE SPHRANTZES

Research on the fall of Constantinople in 1453 depends on diaries or accounts written shortly after the Ottoman Turks conquered the city. It is particularly difficult to get an unbiased opinion of what happened since those witnessing the events wrote accounts designed to satisfy the victorious sultan or incite nobility and clergy in Europe to come to the aid of the conquered Byzantines.

Each of the three primary sources used in the research of this book comes with its own limitations. The diary of Nicolo Barbaro is the account of a Venetian who arrived in Constantinople as a ship's doctor shortly before the siege of the city and left immediately after the Ottoman victory. Well educated and a keen observer, Barbaro seems to have made entries in his diary each day, and his description of the siege is considered accurate. However, he has an outsider's narrow perspective of Byzantine politics and culture.

A Greek chronicler named Kritovoulos, or Critobulos, who lived during the conquest, wrote a history of Turkish military exploits from 1451 through 1467. His book seems to be written primarily as propaganda in favor of the Constantinople's conqueror, Mehmed II.

The third primary source is the autobiography of George Sphrantzes. This account was originally written in Greek as it was spoken in the fifteenth century. It was first translated into English by Marios Philippides, a classics professor at the University of Massachusetts at Amherst, an expert in late

Byzantine history, and published in 1980. Here are the starting and ending paragraphs:

I am George Sphrantzes the pitiful First Lord of the Imperial Wardrobe, presently known by my monastic name Gregory. I wrote the following account of the events that occurred during my wretched life. It would have been fine for me not to have been born or to have perished in childhood. Since this did not happen, let it be known that I was born on Tuesday, August 30, 6909.

. . .

I wrote this account at the request of certain prominent individuals in Corfu [Kerkira], who insisted that I should relate the events I have witnessed and in which I have participated. So I completed this account in my own hand and gave it to Lord Antonios, the respected priest. If certain events have been omitted, I will only beg forgiveness, as old age and infirmity did not allow me to finish my work properly. This account was finished on March 29, 6989.

George Sphrantzes (or Phrantzes, a variation of Francis) was a high-ranking government official who served the last three emperors of Byzantium in several capacities, including as a regional governor, ambassador, and personal adviser.

Sphrantzes witnessed the siege of and battle for Constantinople and was sold into slavery by the Turks when the city fell. After gaining freedom for himself and his wife, he became a monk on the island of Corfu and wrote his autobiography from memory. It is likely that whatever diaries or journals he might have written earlier in his life were destroyed when Constantinople was conquered.

Sphrantzes calls himself head of the "imperial wardrobe" (*vestiarion*), which means much more than being in charge of the emperor's clothes and jewels. He was likely in charge of the treasury as well. We see the connection in words such as *vest* (an article of clothing), *investiture* (to install in office), and *investment* (to use money to make a profit).

Sphrantzes uses the Byzantine calendar system, which counted from the beginning of the world—about 5508 B.C.—and started each year on September 1. Thus the year of his birth, 6909, is 1401, according to the modern calendar.

For centuries people believed that Sphrantzes had written two accounts of his life—a shorter version called *Chronicon Minus* (Minor Chronicle) and a longer version called *Chronicon Maius* (Major Chronicle). The beginning and ending of the *Chronicon Minus* is what you see quoted here. The *Chronicon Maius* has more detail, particularly about the siege of Constantinople, but experts in Byzantine literature have concluded that Sphrantzes did not write it. The longer account was written decades after his death by Makarios Melissenos (or Melissourgos), a priest who fled to Naples from a Greek-Venetian island conquered by the Turks. He forged several documents there, including the expansion of Sphrantzes' original book. *Chronicon Maius* is mainly a Greek translation and paraphrasing of a Latin text written by Leonardo Giustiniani, a bishop who witnessed the siege of Constantinople. This book became highly popular among Greeks in Europe and the former Byzantine Empire.

Accuracy is also a concern in the account written by Sphrantzes, as is true for most primary sources of this kind. As the author himself tells us, he is relying on his memory, which might have been faulty. His account also reveals personal biases in favor of some Byzantine leaders—particularly Emperor Constantine XI—and against other leaders, such as the emperor's brothers and a key official named Lucas Notaras. However, many of the events related in the book agree with other sources written at the same time.

TIMELINE

CA. 600 B.C.   Byzas and other Greeks found Byzantion (later called Constantinople).

339 B.C.   Philip II of Macedonia (father of Alexander the Great) fails to conquer Byzantion.

A.D. 100s   Christianity becomes an important religion.

325   Constantine I presides over worldwide council of Christian churches, meeting in Nicaea (present-day Iznik), to establish the Nicene Creed.

330   Constantine I officially dedicates Constantinople as a Christian city and the capital of the Roman Empire.

527–565   Justinian I rules the Byzantine Empire.

600s   Islam becomes an important religion.
Greek fire is invented.

1054   The Roman and Orthodox churches formally split.

1204   Members of the Fourth Crusade capture Constantinople.

1261   Byzantines recapture Constantinople.

1347   The Black Plague kills many in Constantinople.

1395–1402	Turks blockade Constantinople.
1402	Tatars defeat Ottomans and then allow Ottomans to regain power.
1422	Turks attempt an unsuccessful siege of Constantinople.
1449	Constantine XI is crowned emperor of Byzantium.
1451	Mehmed II becomes sultan after his father's death.
1453	Mehmed II captures Constantinople. England and France end Hundred Years War.
1481	Mehmed II dies. His solders withdraw from their march on Rome.
1492	Columbus sails west and finds the Americas.
1520–1566	Ottoman sultan Suleyman I reigns. The Ottoman Empire is at its peak.
1821–1832	Greeks rise up against the Ottomans. European nations protect the independence of Greece.
1826	Ottomans abolish the janissary system after more than four hundred years.
1923	The Republic of Turkey is established.

WHO'S WHO?

CONSTANTINE I (CA. 274–337) The son of a Roman general, Constantine defeated his rivals to become the leader of the Roman Empire. He transferred the capital of the empire from Rome to Byzantium—renamed Constantinople in his honor. He decreed that Christianity would be the official religion of the empire. Constantine's mother, the empress Helena, is said to have unearthed a relic of the True Cross in Jerusalem in 327. She later was named a saint of the Catholic Church.

CONSTANTINE XI PALAEOLOGUS (1404–1453) Constantine XI was the last emperor of Constantinople before it fell to the Ottoman Turks. Constantine came to the throne after his brother, Emperor John VIII, died in 1448. His mother, Helena, was a Serbian princess. Constantine tried unsuccessfully to heal the rift between the Catholic and Orthodox Christian churches. He also tried to protect Constantinople against the Ottoman Turks and probably died defending the city.

JUSTINIAN I (483–565) Born Flavius Petrus Sabbatius in a small village near Skopje (the modern capital of the Republic of Macedonia), Justinian I joined the army under the command of his uncle, Justin, later an emperor of Byzantium. Justin educated Justinian, who rose through the military ranks and then became emperor in 527. Justinian restored to the empire some of the territories previous Roman emperors had held, codified the Roman laws, and rebuilt much of Constantinople after suppressing a revolt against his rule.

MEHMED II (1432–1481) Nicknamed Fatih (the Conqueror), Mehmed II was the sultan of the Ottoman Empire from 1444 to 1446 and from 1451 to 1481. He is best known for capturing Constantinople in 1453. Mehmed extended Ottoman rule east of that city into other Turkish territories in Anatolia and west into the Balkans where he was stopped near Belgrade, capital of Serbia. Mehmed appointed a Greek Orthodox patriarch to help govern Constantinople, which he revitalized, renamed Istanbul, and turned into the capital of the Ottoman Empire.

POPE NICHOLAS V (1397–1455) Tomaso Parentucelli, who became Pope Nicholas V, was born in Italy and studied theology in Bologna. A well-known scholar, he became bishop of Bologna and helped in diplomatic negotiations with religious leaders in Germany. After becoming pope in 1447, he strove to restore and rebuild Rome, improve the city's water supply, and support culture and the arts. But his good works were overshadowed by the fall of Constantinople in 1453 and his unsuccessful attempts to launch a crusade afterward. His last years as pope were bitter ones, and he died in 1455.

ROXELANA (CA. 1510–1558) The daughter of an Orthodox priest in the Ukraine, Aleksandra Lisowska became a favorite slave of Ottoman sultan Suleyman I. She was also known as Roxelana and Hurrem (Turkish for "laughing one"). Suleyman married her, and she used her position and skills to make sure that one of her sons would be the next sultan. Roxelana was active in politics and foreign affairs, and she was the first woman to endow a mosque. She died eight years before Selim II, the least capable of her sons, took the throne.

GEORGE SPHRANTZES (1401–1477) A Byzantine diplomat, government official, and adviser to Constantine XI, George Sphrantzes strove to keep the peace between the people of Constantinople and the Ottomans. He was captured during the fall of Constantinople but was able to buy his freedom and later retired to a monastery in Corfu, an island administered by Venice. There he wrote his autobiography, from which historians have learned much about what happened during the last years of the Byzantine Empire.

SULEYMAN I (1494–1566) The great-grandson of Mehmed II, Suleyman brought the Ottoman Empire to its peak of power. The riches and beauty of Istanbul earned him the nickname Suleyman the Magnificent. Influenced by his Ukrainian wife, Roxelana, he killed his grand vizier and the most able of his sons (by another wife). During his reign, from 1520 to 1566, he expanded the Ottoman Empire, rebuilt the walls of Jerusalem, fought corruption within his government, supported the arts, and reconstructed the Ottoman system of law.

THEODORA (CA. 500–548) The wife of Byzantine emperor Justinian I and joint ruler of the empire, Theodora was born into a lower-class family of entertainers. Her strong leadership helped quell the Nika Revolt against the emperor. She advanced the rights of women and tried to heal the rift between Christian sects. Like Justinian, Theodora is venerated as a saint in the Orthodox Church.

TIMUR THE TATAR (1336–1405) Also known as Tamerlane, or Tamberlane (from the Persian Timur-i-lenk meaning "Timur the Lame"), Timur claimed to be a descendant of Genghis Khan, who had unified the Mongols in the early thirteenth century. Timur conquered a vast area from southern Russia to India and Persia and westward through the Anatolian Peninsula. Timur's army later withdrew from Anatolia to prepare for an invasion of China.

GLOSSARY

BASHI-BAZOUKS: Mehmed's irregular army consisting of poorly tried, self-armed peasants, who were the first to attack the walls of Constantinople

BLACK DEATH: the name for the disease, thought to be bubonic plague, that spread through Asia and Europe in the 1300s killing millions

BYZANTINE EMPIRE: the eastern half of the Roman Empire after the fall of the Western Roman Empire in A.D. 476. Its name came from the ancient Greek city of Byzantium.

BYZANTION: the Greek's name for what became Constantinople. Greeks settled the city in about 650 B.C. naming it after their leader, Byzas.

CALIPH: a leader or ruler of the Islamic religion and people. In the Middle Ages, Muslims lived in caliphates (territories ruled by a caliph). Caliph also means "successor" in Arabic and can refer to a religious leader.

CODEX: a ten-volume set of updated laws introduced under the Emperor Justinian I

CRUSADERS: armies of European volunteers who, in the twelfth and thirteenth centuries, went to regain control of Jerusalem and the holy lands of the Bible from Arabic conquerers

DEMES: self-governing groups within Constantinople. The citizens were divided into four groups and assigned civic duties around the city.

DEVSHIRME: "gathering" in Turkish. The name was given to the boys taken from Christian families and educated for service to the sultan.

EUNUCHS: men who had their testicles removed. These men were able to rise to power in Byzantine society.

GOLDEN HORN: the name of the deep-water harbor at Constantinople

GREAT SCHISM: the final break between the Roman Catholic and Greek Orthodox Churches in 1054

HOLY ROMAN EMPIRE: ruled by the Hapsburg family and originating in Austria, the Holy Roman Empire gained dominance over parts of Europe as the Ottoman Empire was also expanding

ISLAM: a religion founded by the prophet Muhammad, after he had experienced a revelation from God through the angel Gabriel. Islam means "submission to God" in Arabic.

JANISSARIES: the new corps (yeniceri) of troops organized by the sultan Murad. The first janissaries were prisoners of war.

MERCENARIES: paid soldiers, not loyal to any particular country or group

MILLET: a self-governing community within the Ottoman Empire. The Greek Orthodox patriarch controlled such a millet.

NIKA REVOLT: rioters shouting "Nika! (victory)" raged through Constantinople protesting emperor Justinian's repression. Justinian wanted to flee the city, but was convinced by his wife Theodora to stay and fight. He put down the revolt, which cost at least 30,000 lives.

ORTHODOX CHRISTIANS: those Christians found in the East (Greece, Turkey, Russia) who are part of the Eastern Orthodox Church and not the Western Church centered in Rome

OTTOMAN EMPIRE: founded in Anatolia in the 1300s, and lasting into the twentieth century, the Ottomans were one of the most powerful empires of their time. Ruled by sultans, they controlled territory across Europe and North Africa, captured the city of Constantinople, and spread Islamic religion and culture throughout the empire.

QUAESTOR: top legal officer in the Roman Empire

ROMAN CATHOLIC CHURCH: ruled by the Pope in Rome, the Roman Catholic Church is the center of Western Catholicism around the world

ROMAN EMPIRE: originating in the first century B.C., the Roman Empire controlled area from Europe to the Middle East and Africa and was the most powerful empire of its day.

VIZIER: a high government official in Islamic governments, especially in the Ottoman Empire

ZIMMI: a term for protected people. Christian and Jews who paid taxes were protected from persecution in the Ottoman Empire under Mehmed.

SOURCE NOTES

4   Bernard Lewis, *Istanbul and the Civilization of the Ottoman Empire* (Norman: University of Oklahoma Press, 1963), 26–27.

5   Philip Mansel, *Constantinople: City of the World's Desire, 1453–1924* (New York: St. Martin's Press, 1995), xi.

5   Ibid.

12 John Julius Norwich, *A Short History of Byzantium* (New York: Vintage Books, 1997), 64.

13 Ibid., 66.

21 Crane Brinton, John B. Christopher, and Robert Lee Wolff, *A History of Civilization, Prehistory to 1715*, vol. 1, 2nd ed. (Englewood Cliffs, NJ: Prentice-Hall, 1960), 243–244.

22 Ibid., 239.

28 Geoffrey of Villehardouin, *La conquête de Constantinople*, ed. Edmond Faral, quoted in Donald E. Queller and Thomas F. Madden, *The Fourth Crusade: The Conquest of Constantinople*, 2nd ed. (Philadelphia: University of Pennsylvania Press, 1997), 155.

30 Norwich, 240.

38 Geoffrey of Villehardouin, quoted in Queller and Madden, 83.

41 Ibid., 182.

41 Ibid., 178.

42 Ibid.

43 Norwich, 304, 305.

49 Ibid., 317.

50 Kosovo.net, "The Battle of Kosovo: Serbian Epic Poems," *Kosovo.net*, (1999) http://www.kosovo.net/sk/history/battle_of_kosovo.html #s02. (October 31, 2007).

66 Steven Runciman, *The Fall of Constantinople 1453* (Cambridge, UK: Cambridge University Press, 1965), 1.

72 Lewis, 47.

74 George Sphrantzes, *The Fall of the Byzantine Empire: A Chronicle by George Sphrantzes: 1401–1477*, trans. Marios Philippides (Amherst: University of Massachusetts Press, 1980), 50.

76 Sphrantzes, 49, 50.

78 Ibid., 57.

78 Ibid., 59.

79 Ibid.

79 Runciman, 63–64.

82	Sphrantzes, 72.
84	Runciman, 74.
85	Nicolo Barbaro, *Diary of the Siege of Constantinople 1453*, trans. J. R. Jones (New York: Exposition Press, 1969), 25.
85–86	Ibid.
86	Sphrantzes, 69.
88	Barbaro, 54.
88	Barbaro, 33.
89	Ibid., 36.
90	Ibid., 46.
90	Ibid., 32.
91–92	Ibid., 52.
93	Ibid., 56.
93	Kritovoulos, 80.
97	Ibid., 63.
100	Ibid., 67.
100–101	Mansel, 1.
102	Kritovoulos, *History of Mehmed the Conqueror*, trans. Charles T. Riggs (Westport, CT: Greenwood Press, 1970), 93.
103	Sphrantzes, 74.
103	Ibid., 75.
104	Barbaro, 61.
109	Lewis, 100.
109	Ibid., 101.
110	Mansel, 11.
111	Sphrantzes, 89.
124	Runciman, 160.
129	John Freely, *Istanbul: The Imperial City* (New York: Viking, 1996), 297.
130	W. E. H. Lecky, *History of European Morals from Augustus to Charlemagne*, vol. 2 (New York: D. Appleton and Company, 1879), 13–14, quoted in Brinton, 2:212.
133–134	Sarah Delaney, "On First Trip, Benedict Urges Unity," *Washington Post*, May 30, 2005, A15.
135	Mansel, 3.
135	Ibid., 7.

SELECTED BIBLIOGRAPHY

PRIMARY SOURCES

Barbaro, Nicolo. *Diary of the Siege of Constantinople 1453*. Translated by
J. R. Jones. New York: Exposition Press, 1969.

Kritovoulos. *History of Mehmed the Conqueror*. Translated by Charles T.
Riggs. Westport, CT: Greenwood Press, 1970.

Sphrantzes, George. *The Fall of the Byzantine Empire: A Chronicle by
George Sphrantzes: 1401–1477*. Translated by Marios Philippides.
Amherst: University of Massachusetts Press, 1980.

SECONDARY SOURCES

Brinton, Crane, John B. Christopher, and Robert Lee Wolff. *A History of
Civilization, Prehistory to 1715*. Vol. 1. 2nd ed. Englewood Cliffs, NJ:
Prentice-Hall, 1960.

Goffman, Daniel. *The Ottoman Empire and Early Modern Europe*.
Cambridge, UK: Cambridge University Press, 2002.

Haldon, John. *Byzantium at War: AD 600–1453*. Oxford, UK: Osprey
Publishing, 2002.

Inalcik, Halil, and Donald Quataert. *An Economic and Social History of
the Ottoman Empire, 1300–1914*. Cambridge, UK: Cambridge
University Press, 1994.

Lewis, Bernard. *Istanbul and the Civilization of the Ottoman Empire*.
Norman: University of Oklahoma Press, 1963.

Lowry, Heath. *The Nature of the Early Ottoman State*. Albany: State
University of New York Press, 2003.

Mansel, Philip. *Constantinople: City of the World's Desire, 1453–1924*.
New York: St. Martin's Press, 1995.

McCarthy, Justin. *The Ottoman Turks: An Introductory History to 1923*.
New York: Addison Wesley Longman, 1997.

Nicol, D. M. *The End of the Byzantine Empire*. New York: Holmes &
Meier, 1979.

Norwich, John Julius. *A Short History of Byzantium*. New York: Vintage Books, 1997.

Queller, Donald E., and Thomas F. Madden. *The Fourth Crusade: The Conquest of Constantinople*. 2nd ed. Philadelphia: University of Pennsylvania Press, 1997.

Rautman, Marcus. *Daily Life in the Byzantine Empire*. Westport, CT: Greenwood Press, 2006.

Runciman, Steven. *Byzantine Civilization*. New York: Meridian Books, 1956.

————— *The Fall of Constantinople 1453*. Cambridge, UK: Cambridge University Press, 1965.

FURTHER READING AND WEBSITES

BOOKS

Bator, Robert. *Daily Life in Ancient and Modern Istanbul*. Minneapolis: Lerner Publications Company, 2000.

Behnke, Alison. *The Conquests of Alexander the Great*. Minneapolis: Twenty-First Century Books, 2008.

—————. *The Conquests of Genghis Khan*. Minneapolis: Twenty-First Century Books, 2008.

Biel, Timothy Levi. *The Crusades*. San Diego: Lucent Books, 1995.

Childress, Diana. *Johannes Gutenberg and the Printing Press*. Minneapolis: Twenty-First Century Books, 2008.

—————. *Marco Polo's Journey to China*. Minneapolis: Twenty-First Century Books, 2008.

DiPiazza, Francesca. *Turkey in Pictures*. Minneapolis: Twenty-First Century Books, 2005.

Hamilton, Janice. *The Norman Conquest of England*. Minneapolis: Twenty-First Century Books, 2008.

Hilliam, Paul. *Medieval Weapons and Warfare: Armies and Combat in Medieval Times*. New York: Rosen Publishing Group, 2004.

MacDonald, Fiona, and Mark Bergin. *A 16th Century Mosque*. New York: Peter Bedrick Books, 1994.

Markel, Rita J. *The Fall of the Roman Empire*. Minneapolis: Twenty-First Century Books, 2008.

Ruggiero, Adriane. *The Ottoman Empire*. New York: Benchmark Books, 2003.

WEBSITES

Internet Medieval Sourcebook
http://www.fordham.edu/halsall/sbook.html
The Internet Medieval Sourcebook is located at the Fordham University Center for Medieval Studies.

Medieval Sourcebook
http://www.fordham.edu/halsall/basis/535institutes.html#I.%20Justice%20and%20Law
The Fordham University Center for Medieval Studies also has the Code of Justinian.

The Sultans
http://www.theottomans.org/english/family/selim2.asp
Information on the Ottoman Empire is available at this site.

INDEX

ABOUT THE AUTHOR

Ruth Tenzer Feldman is an award-winning author of biographies and history books, including *Don't Whistle in School: A History of America's Public Schools*. A former attorney and student of international relations, Feldman has lived in Italy and the Netherlands. She now enjoys life in Portland, Oregon, with her faithful pooch, trusty computer, and steadfast husband.

PHOTO ACKNOWLEDGMENTS

The images in this book are used with the permission of: © North Wind Picture Archives, pp. 6, 9 (left); © Kean Collection/Archive Photos/Getty Images, p. 7; © Hulton Archive/Getty Images, pp. 9 (right), 128; The Art Archive/Museo Civico Cristiano Brescia/Dagli Orti, p. 11; The Granger Collection, New York, pp. 18, 73; © Visuals Arts Library (London)/Alamy, p. 19; The Art Archive/ Dagli Orti, p. 20; © Erich Lessing/Art Resource, NY, pp. 21, 44, 86; © Time & Life Pictures/Getty Images, p. 23; The Art Archive/Biblioteca Nazionale Palermo/Dagli Orti, p. 27; © Edinburgh University Library, Scotland, With kind permission of the University of Edinburgh/The Bridgeman Art Library, p. 29; © Werner Forman/Art Resource, NY, p. 30; The Art Archive/Bibliothèque des Arts Décoratifs Paris/Dagli Orti, p. 33; © Roger-Viollet/The Image Works, pp. 35, 60, 65, 75, 97, 113; © Cameraphoto/Art Resource, NY, p. 37; © Scala/Art Resource, NY, p. 42; © Laura Westlund/Independent Picture Service, pp. 48, 123; © Archivo Iconografico, S.A./CORBIS, p. 51; © Stapleton Collection, UK/The Bridgeman Art Library, p. 53; The Art Archive/Museo Correr Venice/Dagli Orti (A), p. 59; © Mary Evans Picture Library/The Image Works, pp. 63, 91; © Worcester Art Museum, Massachusetts, USA/Jerome Wheelock Fund/The Bridgeman Art Library, p. 67; © Snark/Art Resource, NY, p. 68; The Art Archive/British Library, p. 70; The Art Archive/Turkish and Islamic Art Museum Istanbul/Dagli Orti (A), p. 74; © Yann Arthus-Bertrand/CORBIS, pp. 80, 120; © Topham/The Image Works, pp. 95, 100; © Geoffrey Clements/ CORBIS, p. 108; © Private Collection/Archives Charmet/The Bridgeman Art Library, p. 112; © National Gallery Collection; By kind permission of the Trustees of the National Gallery, London/CORBIS, p. 115; © Christie's Images/CORBIS, p. 118; The Art Archive/Mohammed Khalil Museum Cairo/Dagli Orti, p. 119; © Vanni/Art Resource, NY, p. 121; © Stapleton Collection/CORBIS, p. 125; © Underwood & Underwood/CORBIS, p. 126; © Bettmann/CORBIS, p. 131; © Gianni Giansanti/CORBIS, p. 134.

Cover: © Erich Lessing/Art Resource, NY.